Easy HyperStudio®

Projects That Fit
Right Into Your Curriculum

BY JORDAN D. BROWN

**10 Super-Cool Projects With Step-by-Step Reproducible Directions
That Use the Power of *HyperStudio* to Motivate All Kids
and Liven Up Learning!**

SCHOLASTIC
PROFESSIONAL BOOKS

New York • **Toronto** • **London** • **Auckland** • **Sydney**

DEDICATION

To my wife, Ellen, whose love, humor, and friendship I cherish.

Acknowledgments

Lucky for me, the first *HyperStudio* expert I met was Glenn H. Rustay, a creative 5th-grade teacher at Garden City Elementary School in Florida. Along with Diane Barber-Lacroix, Glenn offered suggestions and technical know-how to help this book immeasurably. In addition, his students piloted these multimedia projects. Screenshots of their terrific stacks can be found on the On the Computer pages.

Maria L. Chang, I'm in awe of your talents as an editor. Your thoughtful comments and inspired ideas improved these projects enormously.

Thanks to Liza Charlesworth for introducing me to Glenn and for helping with the early stages of this book. Of course, if Terry Cooper had never asked me to write this book in the first place, I'd probably still be in the dark about the splendors of *HyperStudio*.

Eileen and Stephen Brown are not only amazing teachers, but awesome parents.

Satchmo, my cocker spaniel pal, valiantly put up with my loud typing while he was trying to snooze at my feet.

Jordan D. Brown
New York City, 2001

The wonderful screenshots in this book were all created by
Mr. Rustay and his very talented students.
Many thanks to Francesca A., Jorge A., Tiffany B., Shari C., Lauren D., Willkecia E.,
Daniel F., Kara F., Jack F., Hilda G., Cynthia G., Elisea G., Brandi H., Chauncey H.,
Kennethia J., Logan J., Michael L., James L., Shantera L., Daniel L., Lizbeth M., Amanda M.,
Lauren M., Darrah O., Zacharias P., Keona S., Thomas S., and Jose T.

Cover and interior design
by Holly Grundon

ISBN: 0-439-13114-6

HyperStudio® is a registered trademark of Knowledge Adventure, Inc.

CONTENTS

Introduction 4

Getting the Most Out of This Book 5

Assessing *HyperStudio* Projects 6

10 Easy HyperStudio Projects

1 **About Me** *(Language Arts)* 8

2 **Create-a-Mystery** *(Language Arts)* 14

3 **Biography** *(Social Studies, Language Arts)* 21

4 **Book Report** *(Language Arts)* 29

5 **Endangered Species Report** *(Science, Math)* 37

6 **State Brochure** *(Social Studies, Language Arts)* 48

7 **Early Explorer Report** *(Social Studies)* 59

8 **Space Exploration Timeline** *(Science, Social Studies)* . . . 69

9 **Math Story and Quiz** *(Math, Language Arts)* 79

10 **Class Yearbook** *(Language Arts)* 87

"Hey, These Cards Are Stacked!" and Other *HyperStudio* Wonders

You may already have heard teachers and principals raving about the benefits of using *HyperStudio* in the classroom. This popular multimedia software helps students with a variety of learning styles create interactive presentations on the computer that demonstrate their knowledge of curriculum content.

These *HyperStudio* presentations (called "stacks") usually contain several on-screen cards with buttons, graphics, sounds, animation, and other multimedia effects. As students work cooperatively in pairs or small groups to create projects in *HyperStudio*, they develop critical-thinking skills and communication skills, and become more proficient at collaborating with other students and revising their work. *HyperStudio* can also be an effective motivating tool for students who find traditional writing projects frustrating.

This book was designed for busy teachers who would like to start using *HyperStudio* in their classroom, but don't know where to begin. It was also written for teachers who worry that the "bells and whistles" of *HyperStudio* will interfere with their curriculum. For this reason, each project in this book focuses primarily on one or more curricular areas. Any multimedia effects that are not directly tied to the curricular goals are described at the end of the lesson.

How the Projects Are Organized

Each project is divided into 4 sections:

1 **For the Teacher** – This page includes a summary of the project, plus a list of preparations, and a lesson plan.

2 **Planning Pages** – These reproducible pages give students a summary of the project and provide a detailed framework for organizing their thoughts before they build the stack on the computer.

3 **On the Computer instructions** – This step-by-step reproducible takes students through the process of creating each project on *HyperStudio*. Examples of stacks created by 5th-grade students are incorporated, so students have a visual model to work from.

4 **Tips for Improving the Stack** – Once students have successfully completed their stack, they can revise it by trying out some of *HyperStudio's* multimedia tools.

Getting the Most Out of This Book

In creating this book, we used the 3.2 Mac version of *HyperStudio*. All of the screenshots and commands you'll see in this book are specific to Macintosh computers. Except for file names, there's very little difference between the Windows and Macintosh versions of *HyperStudio*. When necessary, we try to provide the file names for both versions.

Learn the Basics First

Projects 1 to 3 (About Me, Create-a-Mystery, and Biography) provide instruction in many of the basic *HyperStudio* skills such as using the tool box, adding text objects, adding buttons, and creating backgrounds. I highly recommend that your students complete Projects 1–3 before moving on to the others. After that, feel free to choose any project that suits your curriculum needs and interests.

Try the Projects Yourself

If you make a sample stack before introducing the project to your class, you will be more aware of the procedure and possible pitfalls. (When you're working with any new software program, it isn't a matter of *if* you'll make mistakes but *when* you'll make them.)

Have Students Work in Pairs or Small Groups

While it's possible for students to create stacks themselves, the process is more enjoyable and rewarding when done in cooperative groups. Ideally, two students work together, although a small group of three can also work well. Students can take turns reading the directions and working on the computer. (For the first project, students work alone to master the basics.)

Make Some Students the Experts

Most likely, you'll have a few tech-savvy kids in your class who can master *HyperStudio* almost immediately. Use them to help other students in need.

Create Student Work Folders on the Computer

At the start of the school year, place a directory on the computer with your name. Under this directory, create a student sub-directory, using students' last names to label work folders. Teach students how to save projects on their own work folders. Also, have them name their project files using their last name followed by the project name (e.g., Brown.Biography).

Give Students Time to Explore *HyperStudio's* Resources

As students start to use *HyperStudio*, they will be curious about the different patterns, clip art, sounds, transitions, and button icons available. Encourage students to click through the different options and make notes about what they like and dislike.

On the next two pages, you'll find a handy assessment guide and reproducible rubric for your students' *HyperStudio* projects. Enjoy the rest of the book!

INTRODUCTION

Assessing *HyperStudio* **Projects**

If you are new to using *HyperStudio*, the task of evaluating students' stacks probably seems daunting. You'll be relieved to learn that assessing *HyperStudio* projects is similar to assessing other kinds of student projects, such as paper reports and oral presentations. First-rate projects are well organized, reflect creativity, are expressed clearly, and use visuals to support the text.

On the following page, you'll find a *HyperStudio* Project Evaluation Form that can help you and your students discuss the merits and drawbacks of their stacks. The scale on this form goes from "1" (poor) to "5" (excellent). This form assesses projects along the following criteria:

Preparation – How well did the student fill out the Planning Pages for the project? Were all the sections completed thoughtfully and carefully?

Collaboration – How successfully did the student collaborate on the project throughout the process? Did the student cooperate and do a fair share of the work?

Curriculum Content – Does the stack reflect the student's knowledge of the topic? Did the student master the educational objectives for this project?

Writing – Did the student express his or her thoughts clearly and in a lively manner? Are the titles clear and concise? Are there any spelling or grammar mistakes? Did the student revise the writing?

Visuals – Is the stack visually appealing? Are there any original drawings? Are the photographs appropriate to the topic? Are the cards neat or cluttered? Did the student choose colors that complement each other?

Navigation – How well organized is the stack? Is it clear what buttons the reader should click? Do all the buttons do what they're supposed to do?

***HyperStudio* Skills –** Did the student follow the directions for the stack? When the student didn't understand something, did he or she ask for help?

I have found that when students are given the assessment criteria at the start of a project, they are more likely to rise to the challenge, persist, and revise their work until their projects are excellent. Students can use this form to give helpful feedback to each other before they submit their projects for final assessment.

Evaluation Form

NAME: _____ DATE: _____

PROJECT: _____

Criteria	Score Poor — Excellent
Preparation *(Planning Pages)*	1 2 3 4 5
Collaboration with Other Students *(cooperation, flexibility)*	1 2 3 4 5
Curriculum Content *(research, organization, creativity)*	1 2 3 4 5
Writing *(clarity, organization, spelling, grammar)*	1 2 3 4 5
Visuals *(graphics, original drawings)*	1 2 3 4 5
Navigation *(buttons, organization of stack, consistency)*	1 2 3 4 5
HyperStudio **Skills** *(followed directions, stack "works")*	1 2 3 4 5
TOTAL SCORE	_____

Comments:

_____

_____

_____

_____

For the Teacher

About Me

In this introduction to *HyperStudio*, students write about their favorite subject—themselves! This single-card project includes a cartoon self-portrait and an autobiographical blurb.

Before Class:

✻ Make a sample About Me card to familiarize yourself with the steps involved, the basic *HyperStudio* tools, and possible pitfalls. Your stack will help motivate students, and provide a model for them.

✻ Gather some examples of biographical blurbs from a variety of sources, such as book jackets, baseball cards, reference books, and Web sites. If possible, find blurbs about people that your students admire.

✻ For each student, photocopy the Planning Page and On the Computer instructions for this project (pages 9–13).

During Class:

✻ Have students read examples of biographical blurbs from the sources you gathered. Discuss the kinds of information that are usually included in these blurbs, such as the person's hometown, family, and hobbies.

✻ Tell students that they will use *HyperStudio* to create their own mini-autobiographies. Show the sample card you created.

✻ If possible, use a computer hooked up to an overhead projector to demonstrate how to start a new stack. Also, show students how to "tear off" the **TOOLS** and **COLORS** menus. First, click on the **TOOLS** menu at the top of the screen. While holding down the mouse button, drag the **TOOLS** to the left side of the card. Repeat with the **COLORS** menu. (Students may have to practice tearing off these menus a few times before they get a feel for it.) Next, click on the **EDIT** menu and point out the **Undo** option, which students can use if they make a mistake.

✻ Distribute copies of the Planning Page and On the Computer instructions. Once you have approved a student's Planning Page, he or she can work on the computer.

✻ Learning the basics of *HyperStudio* can be frustrating. Remind students that learning any new computer program takes practice. If they keep working on it, they'll eventually master the basics.

Planning Page
About Me

Write about one of your favorite topics–YOURSELF!
Use *HyperStudio*'s paint tools to draw a picture of yourself.

Directions:
Write a few paragraphs (about 50–100 words) about yourself. Below are some sentences to help you get started. Have fun!

Hi! My name is _____

and I'm _____ years old. I live in _____

with _____.

I am in the _____ grade at _____

school in _____ (city, state).

My favorite subjects are _____.

My favorite hobbies are _____.

My favorite food is _____.

One of my favorite books is _____

because _____

_____.

I really like _____

_____

_____.

Project 1

On the Computer
About Me

1 Start up *HyperStudio*.

2 From the **FILE** menu at the top, choose **New Stack**, then click OK. You'll see a blank white card.

3 Click and drag the **TOOLS** and **COLORS** menus, and put them on either side of the card.

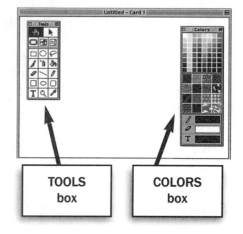

TOOLS
box

COLORS
box

Add a Text Object for the title (see below).

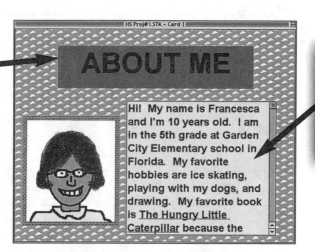

Add a Text Object for your auto-biographical blurb (see below).

Add 2 Text Objects for the title and blurb:

1 From the **OBJECTS** menu, click **Add a Text Object**. Read the help message, then click OK. You'll see a rectangle of red "marching ants" appear on the card.

About Me

2 Put your cursor inside the rectangle, so it becomes a **4-way arrow** ✛ . Click and drag the rectangle to the top of the card.

3 Reshape the rectangle to fit the card's title:

* <u>To make the rectangle wider or thinner</u>, put the cursor on the left or right edge until the cursor turns into **left-right arrows** ↔ . Then, click and drag the edge to where you want it.

* <u>To make the rectangle taller or shorter</u>, put the cursor on the top or bottom edge until the cursor turns into **up-down arrows** ↕ . Then, click and drag the edge to where you want it.

4 Once you're satisfied with the rectangle's size, click outside it. The **Text Appearance** window will appear. Click the **Style** button in the lower left corner. On the **Text Style** window, make the following choices:

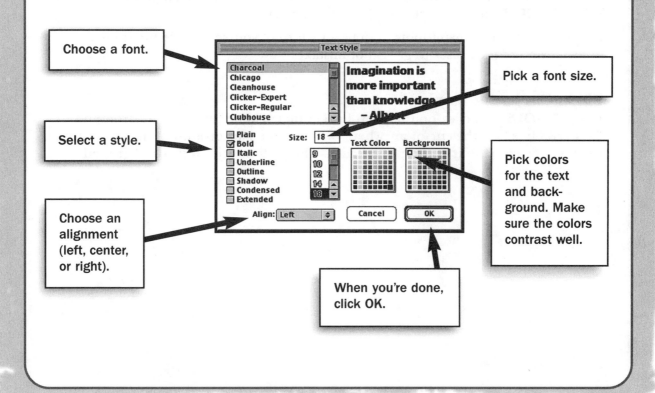

About Me

5 Back on the **Text Appearance** window, click on **Draw scroll bar** and **Scrollable** to remove the check marks. Click OK.

6 Type "ABOUT ME" inside the text object.

7 Repeat Steps 1–4 to create another text object for your autobiographical blurb. (Skip Step 5.) Type in information about yourself.

8 From the **EXTRAS** menu, select **Check Spelling**. Click on **This stack**, and click **Start**. For each word that is questioned, choose either **Replace** or **Skip**.

9 Under the **FILE** menu, click **Save Stack**. Find the folder with your name, then type in a file name for this project and click **Save**.

Draw a picture of yourself:

1 To draw a picture frame, click on the **rectangle tool** in the **TOOLS** box. (See next page.) Click on any color or pattern you like in the **COLORS** box. Position the cursor below and to the left of the title box. Hold down the mouse and drag it diagonally down to the right, then let go. (If you want to change the frame, go to the **EDIT** menu, select **Undo**, and try again.)

2 Use the different **paint tools** to draw a picture of yourself inside the frame. You can use the **eraser** to get rid of mistakes.

Fill in the background:

In the **TOOLS** box, click on the **paint bucket tool**. Then pick a pattern from the **COLORS** box. Put the cursor anywhere on the white background of the card (not on the text objects or your picture), and click. The pattern will fill the background.

On the Computer

About Me

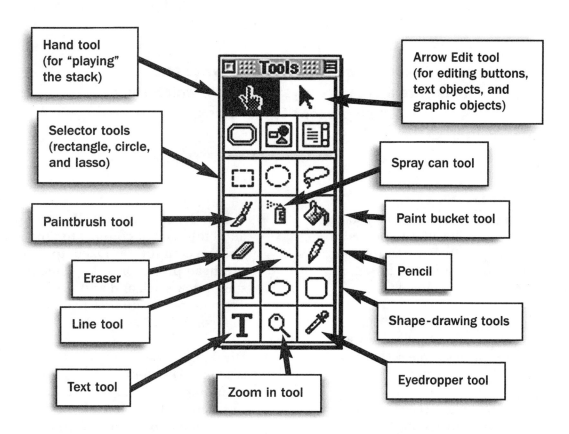

Hand tool (for "playing" the stack)

Arrow Edit tool (for editing buttons, text objects, and graphic objects)

Selector tools (rectangle, circle, and lasso)

Spray can tool

Paintbrush tool

Paint bucket tool

Eraser

Pencil

Line tool

Shape-drawing tools

Text tool

Zoom in tool

Eyedropper tool

TIPS FOR IMPROVING THIS STACK

❋ If you want to change the background pattern, go to the **EDIT** menu, and click **Undo Painting**. Then use the **paint bucket tool** to add a different background. You can also click on **Erase Background** under the **EDIT** menu, but this will also erase anything you drew on the card.

❋ If you want to make a thicker picture frame, double-click the **line tool** and select a wider line. Click the **rectangle tool**, pick a color or pattern, and then draw the frame.

For the Teacher

Create-a-Mystery

Students work in teams to write and illustrate a creative mystery story, which they then present to the class.

Before Class:

✳ Make a sample Create-a-Mystery stack to familiarize yourself with the procedure and possible pitfalls. Your sample stack will help motivate students, as well as provide them with a model.

✳ For each student, photocopy the Planning Pages and On the Computer instructions for this project (pages 15–20).

✳ If possible, gather a few examples of short mystery stories. Pick stories that have good "cliffhangers" (suspenseful events) at the end of sections or chapters.

During Class:

✳ Ask student volunteers to read some short mystery stories aloud. Then discuss the techniques that the author used to build suspense.

✳ Explain to students that they will be working in teams to create short mystery stories using *HyperStudio*. Each student in a team will create one part (and one card) of the story. Present the sample stack you created.

✳ Tell students that they will learn how to add buttons that connect to other cards. Using a computer hooked up to an overhead projector or large monitor, start a new stack and add a second card. Then demonstrate how to add a button that connects these cards.

✳ Divide the class into teams of five students. Distribute copies of the Planning Pages and On the Computer instructions to each student. Once you have approved a team's Planning Pages, students can take turns creating their cards on the computer.

✳ When all the mystery stories are completed, invite each team to present their work to the class. If possible, attach a large monitor to a computer, so the whole class can read the stories together.

Planning Pages
Create-a-Mystery

Collaborate with four classmates to create a short mystery story. You'll learn how to make buttons that readers can click to find out what happens next.

NAMES: _____

_____

_____

_____

_____

Directions:

Write the numbers 1 to 5 on small scraps of paper, then crumple them up. Each student picks a number to learn which of the five cards to work on.

CARD 1: COVER

As a group, brainstorm at least three titles for a short mystery story. Write down all your ideas. Think of titles that tell the setting or the main character in the story, such as *The Mystery at [your school's name]* or *The Ghost of Mr. McFoddle.* Author #1 decides which title the team will use. Write the final title below:

_____

CARD 2: OPENER

Author #2 writes the first part of the story below. In about five sentences, introduce the main character and setting, based on the title. Make the last sentence a suspenseful "cliffhanger," so readers will be eager to read on.

_____

_____

_____

_____

_____

Project 2

Create-a-Mystery

CARD 3: SECOND STORY CARD

Author #3 writes the next part of the story. Pay close attention to what happens at the end of Card 2, so that Card 3 continues the action and suspense. If you want, ask the others on your team for help. Again, end with a "cliffhanger."

_____

_____

_____

_____

_____

CARD 4: THIRD STORY CARD

Author #4 writes the next five sentences of the story. Keep up the suspense, and end with a "cliffhanger."

_____

_____

_____

_____

_____

CARD 5: CONCLUSION

Author #5 writes the conclusion of the story. In about five sentences, explain how the mystery was solved.

_____

_____

_____

_____

_____

On the Computer
Create-a-Mystery

CREATE A NEW STACK

1 Under the **FILE** menu, click on **New Stack**. To add more cards, click **New Card** from the **EDIT** menu four times. The card on the screen should say "Untitled — Card 5" at the top.

2 Go to the **MOVE** menu and select **First Card** to return to Card 1. **Save Stack** in your work folder.

3 Click and drag the **TOOLS** and **COLORS** menus, and put them on either side of the card.

CARD 1: COVER

Add background color. Click on the **paint bucket** in the TOOLS box and pick a color. Then, click anywhere on the card.

The Mystery of the Unwrapped Mummy

Written by
Francesca, Daniel, Lizbeth, Jorge, and Darrah

Next Card

Use the **text tool** to type in the title (see below).

Add a Button that connects to the next card (see p. 18).

Add a Text Object for the authors' names (see p. 18).

Type the title:

1 Double-click the **text tool** ("T") in the **TOOLS** box. In the **Text Style** window, pick a font for your title and a text color that will stand out against your background color. Pick a large size, such as 48 or 72. Click OK.

2 Click your mouse near the upper left corner. Carefully type in your title, leaving room for your names below. If you make a mistake while typing, press the **Delete** key to remove the letters. Press **Return** to start the next line. If you click away from the text, the letters will become part of the background and be difficult to edit.

Create-a-Mystery

Add a Text Object for the authors' names:

1 Under the **OBJECTS** menu, click **Add a Text Object**. Position the rectangle under the title and resize the box to fit your names.

2 Click outside the rectangle to get to the **Text Appearance** window. Click on **Style** and select a medium font size, such as 18 or 24. Pick colors that will stand out against the background, then click OK. Back at the **Text Appearance** window, click on **Draw scroll bar** and **Scrollable** to remove the check marks. Click OK.

3 In the text object, type the names of everyone on your team.

Add a Button that connects to the next card:

1 From the **OBJECTS** menu, select **Add a Button**. When the **Button Appearance** window pops up, type "GO" in the **Name** box.

2 Click on the **Icons** button at the bottom of the screen. Select the ☞ icon in the **Icons** window, then click OK. Click OK again on the **Button Appearance** window.

3 You'll see a button with red "marching ants" around it in the middle of the card. Place the cursor inside this button, hold down the mouse, and drag the button to the lower right-hand corner of the card. Then click outside the button.

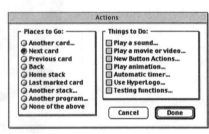

4 When the **Actions** window appears, select **Next card** under **Places to Go**. The **Transitions** window will appear:

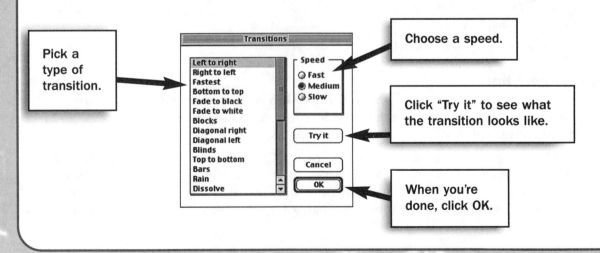

Pick a type of transition.

Choose a speed.

Click "Try it" to see what the transition looks like.

When you're done, click OK.

On the Computer

Create-a-Mystery

5 Back on the **Actions** window, click **Play a sound** under **Things to Do**. The **Tape Deck** window will appear:

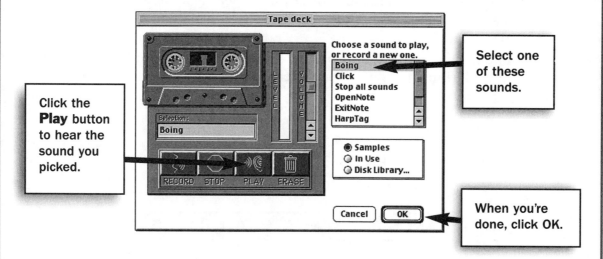

Click the **Play** button to hear the sound you picked.

Select one of these sounds.

When you're done, click OK.

6 Click **Done** in the **Actions** window, and your first button is finished! Try it out. Don't forget to **Save Stack**.

CARD 2: OPENER

Add a Text Object for the story (see below).

Add 2 Buttons that connect to the previous and next cards (see p. 20).

Add a Text Object for your part of the story:
Position and size the rectangle according to the length of your text. Use a font size of 18 or 20. Leave the **Draw scroll bar** and **Scrollable** options checked. Type in the first part of your story. When you're finished typing the text, click on **Check Spelling** under the **EXTRAS** menu.

On the Computer

Create-a-Mystery

Add 2 Buttons that connect to the previous and next cards:

1 **Add a Button** that goes to the **Previous card** (under the **Actions** window). Name the button "Go Back" and pick the ✊ icon. Place the button at the left side of the card.

2 **Add a Button** that goes to the **Next Card** (under the **Actions** window). Name the button "What happens next?" and pick the 👉 icon. Place the button at the right side of the card.

Draw the Scene:

Using the **paint tools**, draw a picture that goes with your part of the story.

CARDS 3–5: OTHER STORY CARDS

For the next three cards, **repeat the steps under Card 2**. Card 5 won't need a "What happens next?" button—it's the end of the story.

TIPS FOR IMPROVING THIS STACK

✳ Want a more dramatic background for your cover card? From the **EDIT** menu, select **Effects**, then choose **Gradients**. In the **Gradients** window, pick two contrasting colors. Then, choose **Circular** or **Rectangular**, and click **Apply**.

✳ To change your button sound to something more dramatic, click on the **arrow edit tool**, then double-click on a button. On the **Button Appearance** window, click **Actions**. Under **Things to Do**, click **Play a sound** twice. Select **Disk Library** on the **Tape Deck** window, and pick one of these suspenseful sounds: **Drama 1**, **Drama 2**, **Harp 1**, **Harp 2**, or **Korg**.

For the Teacher

Biography

Students research a famous person they admire, then write a biography that focuses on the person's childhood and accomplishments. Students incorporate images from the Internet.

Before Class:

✳ Make a sample Biography stack to familiarize yourself with the procedure and possible pitfalls. Your sample stack will help motivate students, as well as provide them with a model.

✳ For each student, photocopy the Planning Pages and On the Computer instructions for this project (pages 22–28).

✳ Invite your school librarian to speak to your students about useful resources to help them write biographies. Students may consult publications such as *Current Biography, Biography Today*, and *Biography* magazine, as well as Internet search engines, and biography Web sites.

During Class:

✳ As a group, ask the class to brainstorm a list of 20 famous people they admire. You may want to suggest categories, such as authors, sports figures, musicians, civil-rights leaders, and actors. Write the names on the board.

✳ Explain to students that they will be working in pairs to create a biography stack in *HyperStudio*. Have students pick a name from the list your class generated. Each pair should write about a different person. Show the sample biography stack you created.

✳ Tell students that they will learn how to copy photographs from the Internet. They'll also learn the time-saving trick of copying and pasting buttons.

✳ Distribute copies of the Planning Pages and On the Computer instructions to each student. Once you have approved a team's Planning Pages, students can create their stack on the computer.

✳ When all the biographies are done, invite volunteers to present their work to the class.

Project 3

Planning Pages

Biography

Work with a partner to create a stack about a famous person you admire. You'll also learn how to copy pictures from the Internet and paste them into your stack.

NAMES: _____

_____

Your Famous Person's Name:

_____

Directions:
Research your famous person in an encyclopedia, books, magazines, or one of the following Web sites:

- http://amillionlives.com
- http://www.biography.com

CARD 1: COVER AND CONTENTS

What years were the person alive? _____

Find a picture of this person on the Internet or an encyclopedia CD-ROM. To save an image from the Internet, click and hold down the mouse button over the picture until a menu pops up. (On a PC, right-click over the image.) Select **Save This Image As…** or **Download Image to Disk**, and save it in your work folder. (Ask your teacher how to copy or save images from encyclopedia CD-ROMs.) Record where you found the image below:

_____

Find a short quote that the person wrote or said:

_____

CARD 2: WHY FAMOUS?

Write a paragraph about what makes this person famous. Why do you admire him or her? What did the person mean by the quote? (If you need more space, write on the back.)

_____

_____

_____

_____

Planning Pages
Biography

CARD 3: CHILDHOOD

Write a paragraph about this person's childhood. Where did he or she grow up? What can
you say about the person's family, friends, hobbies, and heroes?

_____

_____

_____

_____

_____

CARD 4: LIFE-CHANGING EVENT

Write a summary of an important accomplishment or event that happened in this person's life.

_____

_____

_____

_____

_____

CARD 5: BIBLIOGRAPHY

List all books, encyclopedias, Web sites, and other resources you used to learn about this
person. Ask your teacher about what format to use for the bibliography.

_____

_____

CARD 6: ABOUT THE AUTHORS

Write a short description about each of you. (If you need more space, write on the back.)

_____

_____

_____

_____

Project 3

On the Computer
Biography

CREATE A NEW STACK

1   Under the **FILE** menu, start a **New Stack**. Under the **EDIT** menu, click on **New Card** five times to get a total of six cards.

2   Use the **MOVE** menu to return to the **First Card**.

3   Click and drag the **TOOLS** and **COLORS** menus, and put them on either side of the card.

CARD 1: COVER AND CONTENTS

Add a Text Object for name and dates (see below).

Add a Graphic Object of the person's picture (see p. 25).

Add a Button for each of the other cards in this stack (see p. 25).

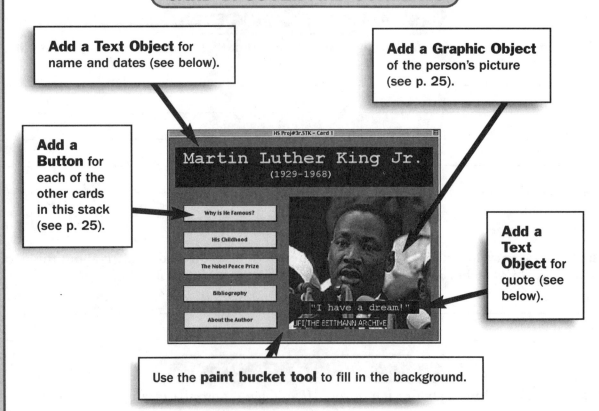

Add a Text Object for quote (see below).

Use the **paint bucket tool** to fill in the background.

Add a Text Object for the person's name and famous quote:

1   Under the **OBJECTS** menu, select **Add a Text Object**. A rectangular box with red "marching ants" will appear. Click inside the box and drag it near the top of the card. Move the cursor to any side of the box to resize it. Then, click outside the box.

On the Computer

Biography

2 In the **Text Appearance** window, click on **Style** and choose a font and font size, as well as text and background colors for the text object. Click OK.

3 Back at the **Text Appearance** window, click on **Draw scroll bar** and **Scrollable** to remove the check marks. Click OK again.

4 Type in your famous person's name and the years he or she was born and died. (If the person is still alive, leave the second year blank, like this: 1975 –   .) To make the font size for the years smaller, click and drag the mouse to highlight the years. Then, go to the **OPTIONS** menu and select **Text Style**. On the **Text Style** window, choose a different font size, then click OK.

5 Repeat Steps 1–3 to **Add a Text Object** for the quote.

Add a Graphic Object of the person's picture:

1 Under the **OBJECTS** menu, select **Add a Graphic Object**. Select your work folder (where you saved your person's image), and double-click on the person's image file. Use the **rectangle selector** to choose the part of the picture you want to use, then click OK.

2 Click and drag the picture to one side of the card. Click outside the picture, then click OK on the **Graphic Appearance** window. To enlarge the picture, click on the **arrow edit tool** in the **TOOLS** box, then click on the picture. When the red "marching ants" surround the picture, hold down the **shift** key and click and drag the corner of the graphic object to resize it.

Add 5 Buttons that connect to the other cards in the stack:

1 Under the **OBJECTS** menu, click **Add a Button**. Name the button "Why is he (or she) famous?" Then click OK.

2 Use the cursor to position the button under the person's name on the card. Keep in mind that you have four more buttons to place there, so make sure you have enough room.

3 Click outside the button to get to the **Actions** window. Under **Places to Go**, select **Another card**. This box will appear:

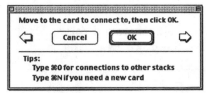

On the Computer

Biography

Click the **right arrow** to select the card you want the button to connect to. For "Why is he (or she) famous?" select Card 2. Pick a transition, then click OK.

4 Back at the **Actions** window, under **Things to Do**, select **Play a sound**. Pick a simple sound, then click OK.

5 Repeat Steps 1–4 four times for the other buttons. Label these buttons "His (or Her) Childhood," "Life-Changing Event," "Bibliography," and "About the Authors." Connect the buttons to Cards 3, 4, 5, and 6, respectively.

6 **Save Stack** in your work folder.

CARD 2: WHY FAMOUS

Add a <u>scrolling</u> Text Object for the main text. (On the Text Appearance window, leave the check marks on Draw scroll bar and Scrollable.)

Draw a picture using the **paint tools**. (Or, **Add a Graphic Object** of a related picture.)

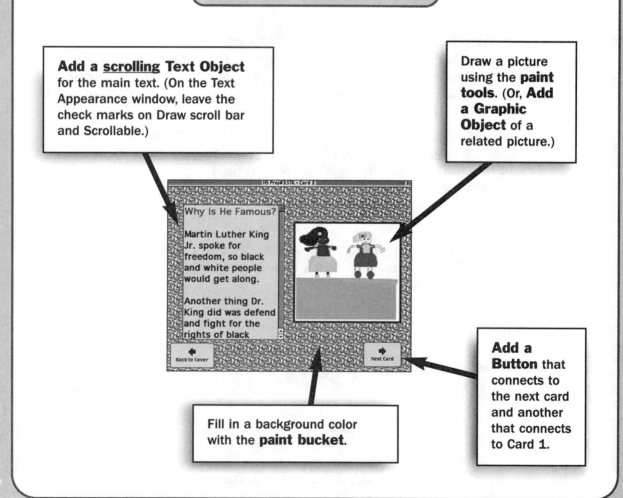

Add a **Button** that connects to the next card and another that connects to Card 1.

Fill in a background color with the **paint bucket**.

On the Computer

Biography

Copy and paste buttons to other cards:

Cards 2, 3, 4, and 5 all need two buttons: one that goes to the next card, and another that goes to Card 1. (Card 6 needs only a button that goes to Card 1.) Instead of making these buttons from scratch, you can copy and paste the two buttons you created on Card 2. Here's how:

1 Click on the **arrow edit** tool, then click on the "Next Card" button. Red "marching ants" will appear around the button. Go to the **EDIT** menu and select **Copy button**.

2 Under the **MOVE** menu, click on **Next Card**. Then, go back to the **EDIT** menu and select **Paste button**.

3 Repeat Step 2 for Cards 4 and 5.

4 Use the **MOVE** menu to **Jump to Card** 2. Repeat Steps 1–3 with the other button (the one that connects to Card 1) for Cards 3 to 6.

5 **Save Stack** in your work folder.

CARDS 3–4

Repeat the steps under Card 2 to create Cards 3 and 4. Type in information about the person's childhood in Card 3, and his or her achievement in Card 4.

CARD 5: BIBLIOGRAPHY

Add a **non-scrolling** Text Object for the title.

Add a **scrolling** Text Object for your resources.

Fill in a background color.

> HS Proj#3r.STK – Card 2
>
> **Bibliography**
>
> We researched Martin Luther King Jr.'s life by using these resources...
>
> The America Encyclopedia.
>
> Great Negro's Past And Present Encyclopedia.
>
> International Library of Negro's Life.
>
> The Negro's Heritage Encyclopedia.
>
> ← Back to Cover   → Next Card

On the Computer

BIOGRAPHY

CARD 6: ABOUT THE AUTHORS

Add a non-scrolling Text Object for the title.

Fill in a background color.

Draw a picture of yourselves using the **paint tools**. (Or, **Add a Graphic Object** for each of your pictures.)

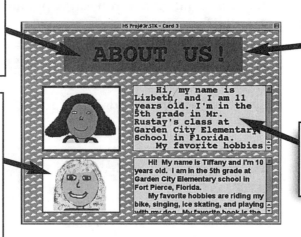

Add a scrolling Text Object for your biographies.

Check Spelling

Under the **EXTRAS** menu, click on **Check Spelling**. On the **Check Spelling** window, select **This stack** to check all the cards at once. Then, **Save Stack**.

TIPS FOR IMPROVING THIS STACK

You can use a graphic object for a button. While on Card 2, click on the **arrow edit tool** and click on the button that connects to Card 1. When the red "marching ants" appear, press the **Delete** button to remove the button. Under the **OBJECTS** menu, **Add a Graphic Object** of the photo you used on the cover. Click and drag the graphic object to where you want it on the card, then click outside the box. In the **Graphic Appearance** window, click on **Actions**. Under **Places to Go**, pick **Another card** to connect the graphic object to Card 1. Click OK, then click **Done** on the **Actions** window. If necessary, click on the **arrow edit tool** to resize the graphic object. You can also copy and paste the graphic object to other cards, the same way you did with the buttons.

For the Teacher

Book Report

**After reading an assigned book, students collaborate
on a *HyperStudio* book report that includes a
plot summary, an annotated character list, a review,
and a biography of the book's author.**

Before Class:

✳ Make a sample Book Report stack to
familiarize yourself with the procedure
and possible pitfalls. Your sample stack
will help motivate students, as well as
provide a model for them.

✳ For each student, photocopy the
Planning Pages and On the Computer
instructions for this project (pages
30–36).

✳ Make a list of books that you think
your students might enjoy reading. You
can get suggestions from your school
librarian or consult the American
Library Association Web site:
http://www.ala.org/yalsa/booklists/
index.html.

During Class:

✳ Explain to students that they will be
working in pairs to create a book report
in *HyperStudio*. Each team will write
about a different book. Show the
sample stack you created. Discuss the
purpose of each section of this report:
characters, summary, review, and author
biography.

✳ Tell students that in this project,
they will learn how to use pre-made
background patterns and add icons
(small pictures) to their buttons.

✳ Distribute copies of the Planning Pages
and On the Computer instructions to
each student. Once you have approved
a team's planning pages, students can
create the stack on the computer.

✳ When all the book reports are done,
invite volunteers to present their stacks
to the class.

Project 4

Planning Pages
Book Report

Together with a partner, read a book, then create a _HyperStudio_ book report.

NAMES: _____

_____

> # Directions:
> Before you read the book, look over the questions on these planning pages, so you'll know what information you'll need for your report.

CARD 1: COVER

Write the following information from the book cover:

TITLE: _____

AUTHOR: _____

Pick an important object from the story. For example, if the story is _Charlie and the Chocolate Factory_, you might choose a chocolate bar. Sketch a picture of this object on the back of this page.

CARD 2: TABLE OF CONTENTS

CARD 3: CHARACTERS

Select three main characters from the book, and write a short description of each. You may wish to list their ages, where they live, their personalities, what they want, and so on. Next to each description, sketch a quick picture of the character.

Character 1:

_____

_____

_____

Book Report

Character 2:

_____

_____

_____

Character 3:

_____

_____

_____

CARD 4: SUMMARY

In a paragraph, tell the plot of the story in your own words. Focus on facts rather than your opinion. Here are some questions to help you:

✳ When and where does the book take place?
✳ Who is the main character? What does he or she want?
✳ What are some obstacles that this character faces?
✳ How does the story end?

_____

_____

_____

_____

_____

_____

Project 4

Book Report

CARD 5: YOUR REVIEW

Write your opinion of the book. What did you like and didn't like about this book? Did you enjoy the story? Did you find any parts disappointing? Would you read another book by this author? Why or why not?

_____

_____

_____

_____

_____

CARD 6: BOOK'S AUTHOR

Write a short biography about the author. You can find some information on the book jacket, an encyclopedia, or the Internet.

_____

_____

_____

_____

_____

CARD 7: ABOUT YOU

Write a short biography about each of you.

_____

_____

_____

_____

_____

On the Computer
Book Report

CREATE A NEW STACK with BOOK BACKGROUND

1 Under the **FILE** menu, start a **New Stack**.

2 Click and drag the **TOOLS** and **COLORS** menus to either side of your card.

3 From the **FILE** menu, select **Import Background**. In the **HS Art** folder, click **Book**, then **Open.**

4 Under the **EDIT** menu, select **Copy Card**. Then, return to the **EDIT** menu and select **Paste Card**. (The background will look the same, but you're now on Card 2.) Select **Paste Card** five more times, until you reach Card 7.

5 Use the **MOVE** menu to return to the **First Card**.

CARD 1: COVER

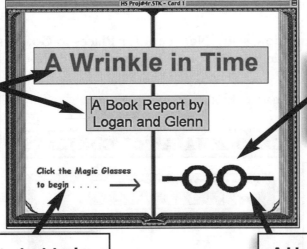

Add a Text Object for the book title and a second one for the report's authors (see p. 34).

Use the **paint tools** to draw an object from the story.

Use the **text tool** to type in instructions for the reader.

Add a Button around the object you drew (see p. 34).

On the Computer

Book Report

Add a Text Object for the title and report authors:

1 Under the **OBJECTS** menu, select **Add a Text Object**. A rectangular box with red "marching ants" will appear. Click inside the box and drag it near the top of the card. Move the cursor to any side of the box to resize it. Then, click outside the box.

2 In the **Text Appearance** window, click on **Style** and choose a font and font size, as well as text and background colors for the text object. Click OK.

3 Back at the **Text Appearance** window, click on **Draw scroll bar** and **Scrollable** to remove the check marks. Click OK again.

4 Type in the title of your book.

5 Repeat Steps 1–3 to **Add a Text Object** for you and your partner's names.

Add a Button (invisible):

1 From the **OBJECTS** menu, select **Add a Button**. On the **Button Appearance** window, choose the **invisible rectangle button**, then click OK.

2 Click and drag the button so that it surrounds the object you drew. Then, click outside the button.

3 On the **Actions** window, select **Next card** for **Places to Go**, pick a transition, and click OK. Under **Things to Do**, pick **Play a sound** and choose a sound. Click OK, then click **Done**.

4 **Save Stack** in your work folder.

CARD 2: TABLE OF CONTENTS

Add a **non-scrolling Text Object** for the card title. (On the Text Appearance window, remove the check marks from Draw scroll bar and Scrollable.)

A Wrinkle In Time

Table of Contents

Characters

Summary

My Review

About the Author

About Me

Add 5 **Buttons** with icons (see p. 35).

On the Computer

Book Report

Add 5 Buttons with Icons:

1 From the **OBJECTS** menu, select **Add a Button**. Choose one of the top four button types.

2 Name the button "Characters," then click OK.

3 Click the **Icons** button. Select an icon to go with the button. You can choose from either the **Samples** or the **Disk Library**. (When the **HS Art** folder appears, click **Icon Library** and **Open**.) Click OK two times.

4 Use the cursor to position the button under your card title. Keep in mind that you have four more buttons to place there, so make sure you have enough room.

5 Click outside the button to get to the **Actions** window. Under **Places to Go**, select **Another card**. Click the **right arrow** on the window to select the card you want the button to connect to. For "Characters," select Card 3. Pick a transition, then click OK.

6 Back at the **Actions** window, select **Play a sound** under **Things to Do**. Pick a simple sound, then click OK. Click **Done**.

7 Repeat Steps 1–6 four times for the other buttons. Label these buttons "Summary," "Our Review," "About [author's name]," and "About Us." Connect the buttons to Cards 4, 5, 6, and 7, respectively.

8 Save Stack.

CARD 3: CHARACTERS

Add a **non-scrolling** Text **Object** for the card title.

Add a **scrolling** Text **Object** for the character list. (Leave the check marks on Draw scroll bar and Scrollable.)

Use the **paint tools** to draw the characters. Use the text tool to type their names.

Add 2 Buttons that connect to the previous and next cards (see p. 36.)

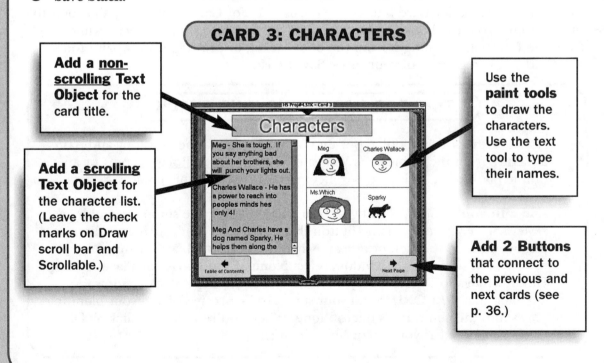

On the Computer
Book Report

Add 2 Buttons that connect to the previous and next cards:

1 From the **OBJECTS** menu, select **Add a Button**.

2 Click **Icons** and select an icon that points left. Click OK two times.

3 Position the button on the lower left-hand corner of the card, then click outside the button.

4 On the **Actions** window, choose **Previous card** for **Places to Go,** and **Play a sound** for **Things to Do**. Click **Done**.

5 Copy and paste the button to the other cards in the stack: Select the **arrow edit tool** in the **TOOLS** box, then click on the button once. From the **EDIT** menu, select **Copy button**. Use the **MOVE** menu to go to **Next Card**. From the **EDIT** menu, click **Paste button**. A new button will appear on this card. Repeat this step for Cards 5–7.

6 Repeat Steps 1–5 to **Add a Button** that connects to the next card. This time, pick an icon that points right. On the **Actions** window, select **Next card** under **Places to Go**. Copy and paste this button on Cards 4–6.

CARDS 4–7

Repeat the steps under Card 3 to create Cards 4–7. For Card 4, use the paint tools to draw a scene from the book. Add a picture of the author on Card 6 by copying it from the Internet, scanning it from the book jacket, or drawing it with paint tools. For Card 7, add a picture of yourselves. **Save Stack**.

TIPS FOR IMPROVING THIS STACK

✱ Add a picture of the book cover on Card 1. Use a scanner, or copy and paste a picture from the publisher's Web site (such as www.scholastic.com) or an online bookstore, such as amazon.com or barnesandnoble.com.

✱ **Add a Button** with a recording of your voice reading the summary and book review. Select an icon for the button that indicates sound, such as a microphone, a stereo speaker, or an ear. Name the button "Hear our summary [or review]." On the **Actions** window, select **None of the Above** for **Places to Go**. Under **Things to Do**, pick **Play a sound**. When the **Tape Deck** window appears, click **RECORD**. Read your summary (or review) from your planning pages into the computer's microphone. When you're finished, click **STOP**. Click **PLAY** to hear your recording. Then click OK.

For the Teacher

Endangered Species Report

**Students research an endangered
animal species, then present their findings
in a report, which features an interactive bar graph.**

Before Class:

✳ Make a sample Endangered Species Report stack to familiarize yourself with the procedure and possible pitfalls. This sample stack will help motivate students, as well as provide a model for them.

✳ For each student, photocopy the Planning Pages and On the Computer instructions for this project (pages 38–47).

✳ Gather books and articles about endangered animal species. You may also want to bookmark the Web sites listed on the Planning Pages.

During Class:

✳ Introduce this project by discussing the terms *species* (a group of animals or plants that share characteristics), *extinction* (what occurs when the last of a species dies), and *endangered species* (a group of animals or plants that are threatened with extinction). Using the research materials you've gathered, ask the class to make a list of some endangered species, such as blue whales, giant pandas, and tigers.

✳ Explain that different animals become extinct for different reasons. Ask: What are some ways in which human actions have caused some animal species to become endangered? *(Some reasons include the destruction of these animals' habitats, pollution, and commercial hunting.)*

✳ Tell students that they will work in pairs to research an endangered animal species of their choice, and then present their findings in a *HyperStudio* stack. (TIP: You may want to limit students to researching animals endangered only in the U.S. Finding population information for endangered animals around the world can be very tricky.) Show the sample stack you created. Discuss the purpose of each of the sections of this report.

✳ Distribute copies of the Planning Pages and On the Computer instructions to each student. Once you have approved a team's Planning Pages, the students can create their stack on the computer.

Project 5

Planning Pages
Endangered Species Report

Every year, thousands of animal species become endangered or extinct because of human actions, such as pollution and hunting. In this project, you and a partner will research an endangered animal species, find out why it is dying out, and learn what can be done to protect it.

NAMES: _____   _____

Directions:

Choose an endangered animal species, then research it in books, encyclopedias, and articles. (You may want to research animals endangered only in the U.S.) Talk with your teacher or librarian about possible resources.

Internet Sites:

http://endangered.fws.gov

http://info.fws.gov

http://eelink.net/EndSpp.old.bak/factsheet.html

http://www.amnh.org/Exhibition/Expedition/Endangered/index.html

http://www.aza.org/programs/ssp

CARD 1: THE COVER

Our endangered animal species: _____

CARD 2: TABLE OF CONTENTS

Find a picture of the animal you chose. You can either scan a picture or download an image from the Internet or a CD-ROM. Save the image in your work folder as a JPG, GIF, or PICT file. Record the source of your image below and the image file name:

_____

Planning Pages

Endangered Species Report

CARD 3: BASIC INFORMATION

Research some basic information about the animal you selected, such as its *appearance* (What does the animal look like?), *habitat* (Where does it live?), *diet* (What does it eat?), and *predators* (What animals, if any, hunt and eat the animal?). Summarize your findings in one or two paragraphs. (If you need more space, write on the back.)

_____

_____

_____

CARD 4: WHY IS IT ENDANGERED?

What are some reasons that the animal species is endangered? What actions can people take to help save this species from extinction? (If you need more space, write on the back.)

_____

_____

_____

CARD 5: ESTIMATED POPULATION BAR GRAPH

Using resources, such as the U.S. Fish and Wildlife Service's Web site, research how your animal's population has changed over the past 20 years. For example, find out your animal's population in 1980, 1985, 1990, and 2000. Or, find out how many animals died each year.

Year   **Estimated Population of the Species Worldwide**

_____   _____

_____   _____

_____   _____

_____   _____

Endangered Species Report

On a separate piece of paper, make a bar graph of this information. On the horizontal x-axis, write the years. On the vertical y-axis, write a range of numbers for the population (in hundreds, thousands, or millions). See example below:

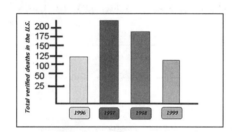

CARD 6: BIBLIOGRAPHY

List all the sources you used to research this project, including books, encyclopedias, Web sites, and interviews. Ask your teacher about what format to use for your bibliography.

_____

_____

_____

_____

_____

CARD 7: ABOUT YOU

Write a paragraph about each of you.

_____

_____

_____

_____

_____

On the Computer
Endangered Species Report

START A NEW STACK

1 Under the **FILE** menu, start a **New Stack**. Under the **EDIT** menu, click on **New Card** six times to get a total of seven blank cards.

2 Use the **MOVE** menu to return to the **First Card**.

3 Click and drag the **TOOLS** and **COLORS** menus to either side of your card.

CARD 1: COVER

Use the **paint tools** to create a background.

Add a Text Object for the title and your names (see below).

Add a Button that takes the reader to the next card (see p. 42).

Add a Text Object:

1 Under the **OBJECTS** menu, select **Add a Text Object**. A rectangular box with red "marching ants" will appear. Click inside the box and drag it near the top of the card. Move the cursor to any side of the box to resize it. Then, click outside the box.

2 In the **Text Appearance** window, click on **Style** and choose a font and a large font size, as well as text and background colors for the text object. Click OK.

3 Back at the **Text Appearance** window, click on **Draw scroll bar** and **Scrollable** to remove the check marks. Click OK again.

4 Type in a title and your names.

On the Computer

Endangered Species Report

Add a Button that connects to the next card:

1 From the **OBJECTS** menu, select **Add a Button**. When the **Button Appearance** window pops up, type something like "Go" or "Next Card" in the **Name** box.

2 Click on the **Icons** button at the bottom of the window, and select an icon. Click OK, then OK again on the **Button Appearance** window.

3 Click and drag the button to the lower right-hand corner of the card. Then, click outside the button.

4 On the **Actions** window, select **Next card** for **Places to Go**. Pick a transition, then click OK. Under **Things to Do**, click **Play a sound**. Select a simple sound, then click OK. Then, click **Done** in the **Actions** window.

5 **Save Stack** in your work folder.

CARD 2: TABLE OF CONTENTS

Add a non-scrolling Text Object for the card title. (On the Text Appearance screen, click on Draw scroll bar and Scrollable to remove the check marks.)

Add 5 Buttons that connect to other cards in the stack (see p. 43).

Add a Graphic Object of your endangered species (see p. 43).

On the Computer

Endangered Species Report

Add a Graphic Object of your endangered species:

1 Under the **OBJECTS** menu, select **Add a Graphic Object**. Select your work folder (where you saved your animal's image), and double-click on the animal's image file. Use the **rectangle selector** to choose the part of the picture you want to use, then click OK.

2 Click and drag the picture to one side of the card. Click outside the picture, then click OK on the **Graphic Appearance** window.

Add 5 Buttons that connect to other cards in the stack:

1 **Add a Button** that connects to another card in the stack. Choose a colored background for your button. Then, name the button "What is a [name of your animal]?" and click OK.

2 Use the cursor to position the button on the card. Keep in mind that you have four more buttons to add, so make sure you have room.

3 Click outside the button to get to the **Actions** window. Under **Places to Go**, select **Another card**. Click the right arrow to select the card you want the button to connect to. For your first button, select Card 3. Pick a transition, then click OK.

4 Back at the **Actions** window, under **Things to Do**, select **Play a sound** for the button and pick a simple sound. Click OK again, then click **Done**.

5 Repeat Steps 1–4 four times for the other buttons. Choose a different color background for each button. Label these buttons "Why is it endangered?", "Estimated Population Graph," "Bibliography," and "About the Authors." Connect them to Cards 4, 5, 6, and 7, respectively.

6 **Save Stack**.

Project 5

On the Computer

Endangered Species Report

CARD 3: BASIC INFORMATION

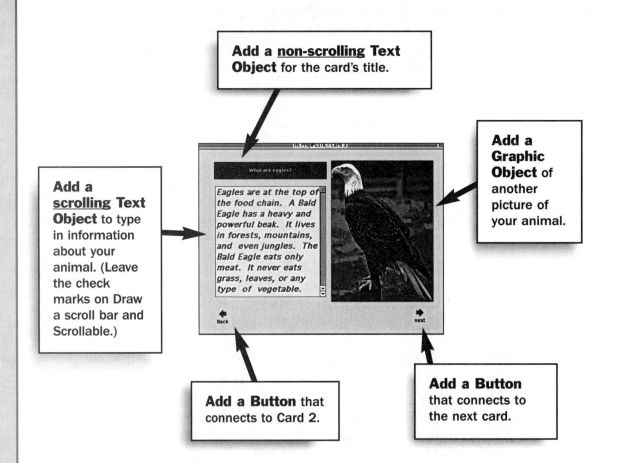

Add a **non-scrolling** Text **Object** for the card's title.

Add a **scrolling Text Object** to type in information about your animal. (Leave the check marks on Draw a scroll bar and Scrollable.)

Add a **Graphic Object** of another picture of your animal.

Add a **Button** that connects to Card 2.

Add a **Button** that connects to the next card.

CARD 4: WHY IS THE SPECIES ENDANGERED?

Repeat the steps under Card 3 to create Card 4.
Copy the "Next" button onto Cards 4 to 6. **Save Stack**.

On the Computer

Endangered Species Report

CARD 5: ESTIMATED POPULATION BAR GRAPH

Use the **text tool** to type instructions for readers.

Use **line** and **text tools** to draw the graph (see below).

Add 4 Text Objects with colored backgrounds to make the graph bars (see below).

Add a Button with HideShow effect (see p. 46).

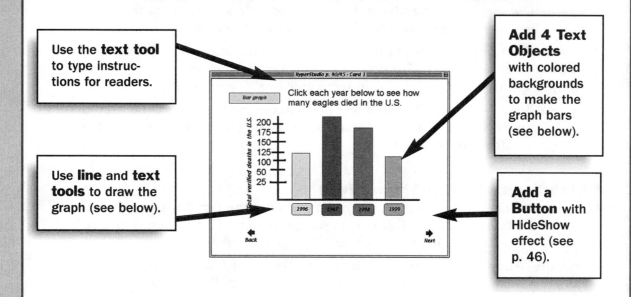

Draw the graph:

1 Use the **line tool** to draw the horizontal and vertical lines of the bar graph. Press the **shift** key as you draw to make straight lines.

2 Use the **text tool** to type in numbers on the y-axis that cover the range of your data. Also, use the **text tool** to label the y-axis "Total population in thousands" (or hundreds or millions). Here's how to turn the text upward:

* Type the text with the **text tool**.

* Click the **rectangle selector tool**, then click and drag the mouse to surround the text. When you release the mouse, you'll see red "marching ants" surround the text.

* Under the **EDIT** menu, go to **Effects**, then select **Scale & Rotate**. Leave the **Scale factor** at 100%. For the **Rotation angle**, enter **90** and select **Counter-clockwise**. Then click OK.

* Click and drag the text to the left of the y-axis of the graph.

Add Text Objects to create bars for the graph:

This may seem confusing at first. Even though you will be adding text objects in this step, you won't be typing any text in them.

On the Computer

Endangered Species Report

1 To make the first bar on your graph, **Add a Text Object** under the **OBJECTS** menu. Use the cursor to reshape the text object into a vertical bar that comes up from the x-axis to the correct height on the y-axis. Click outside the bar.

2 On the **Text Appearance** window, click **Draw scroll bar** and **Scrollable** to remove the check marks. Select a background color. Type in the year of the first bar in your graph (for example, 1980) in the **Name** box. Click OK.

3 Repeat Steps 1–2 to add the other three bars to this graph. Give each bar a different background color. Make sure that you name each text object with the year it goes with in the **Text Appearance** window.

Add Buttons with HideShow effect:

1 **Add a Button** with background color that matches the first bar in your graph. Name the button with the first year in your data (e.g., 1980), then click OK. Position the button under the first bar, then click outside it.

2 On the **Actions** window, select **None of the Above** for **Places to Go**. For **Things to Do**, pick **Play a sound**. In the **Tape Deck** screen, select **Disk Library**, then choose **ScaleHi**, **ScaleMed**, or **StairBonk**.

3 Back at the **Actions** window, click **New Button Actions** under **Things to Do**. This screen will appear:

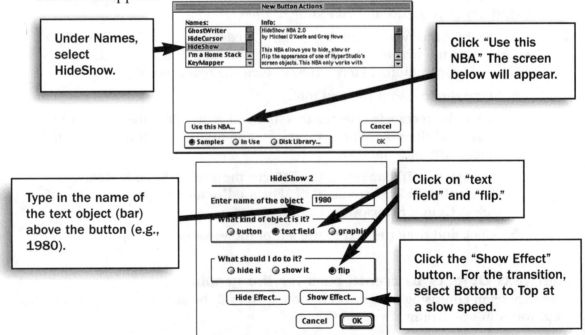

Under Names, select HideShow.

Click "Use this NBA." The screen below will appear.

Type in the name of the text object (bar) above the button (e.g., 1980).

Click on "text field" and "flip."

Click the "Show Effect" button. For the transition, select Bottom to Top at a slow speed.

On the Computer

Endangered Species Report

4 When you're done, click OK here and on the **New Button Actions** window. Then, click **Done** on the **Actions** screen.

5 Repeat Steps 1–4 three more times for the other bars in your graph. For each button, select a background color that matches the bar above it.

6 **Save Stack.**

CARD 6: BIBLIOGRAPHY

Repeat the steps in Card 3 to create Card 6. Type in your resources.

CARD 7: ABOUT THE AUTHORS

Repeat the steps in Card 3 to create Card 7. For your pictures, you can either scan in a photograph or draw yourself using the paint tools.

Check Spelling

Under the **EXTRAS** menu, click on **Check Spelling**. Select **This stack** on the **Check Spelling** window to check all the cards at once. Then, **Save Stack.**

NOTE: Before you present this stack to someone, make sure that all the bars on the graph are hidden. If any bar is visible, click the button below it to hide the bar.

TIPS FOR IMPROVING THIS STACK

❋ You can use some pre-made designs on the *HyperStudio* CD for some of your backgrounds. Under the **FILE** menu, select **Import Background**. In the **HS Art** folder, select **~Media Library** (or **Medialib** in Windows), located on the *HyperStudio* CD. Pick the **Screens & Backgrounds** folder, then choose any design you like.

❋ To help your graphic objects stand out against the background, you can add a frame. When you **Add a Graphic Object**, the **Graphic Appearance** window will appear. In the lower left corner you'll see

| Frame width |
| 0 ⇧ ⇩ |

Click the upper arrow until you see the frame width you like. You can also select any frame color you want.

For the Teacher

State Brochure

Students research one of the 50 states, then present what they've learned in a persuasive *HyperStudio* brochure. This stack includes a clickable map, an interactive timeline, and a list of fun facts that scrolls to music.

Before Class:

✳ Make a sample State Brochure stack to familiarize yourself with the procedure and possible pitfalls. You can use your sample stack as a model for students to follow.

✳ Gather some promotional materials for your state. You can get brochures from your state's tourism department, your local library, or the Internet. You may want to bookmark the Web sites listed on the Planning Pages—they're great resources for state information and digital maps.

✳ For each student, photocopy the Planning Pages and On the Computer instructions for this project (pages 49–58).

During Class:

✳ Show students some promotional materials for your state. Discuss some of the techniques the writers and designers used to persuade tourists to visit the state. Invite students to talk about what they like, what they think could be improved, how graphics help the message, and so on.

✳ Pair up students, and have each pair select a state to research. Each pair will present its findings in a *HyperStudio* stack. Show the sample stack you created.

✳ Distribute copies of the Planning Pages and On the Computer instructions to each team. Once you have approved a team's Planning Pages, the students can create the stack on the computer.

Extension:

✳ After all your students have completed their projects, you can link their stacks under one stack. Create a *HyperStudio* card with a map of the U.S. on it. (You can use the USA clip art in the **HS Art** folder.) Put an invisible button around each of the states the students selected (use the **lasso** to create the button shape). Under **Places to Go** on the **Actions** window, select **Another stack**. When a user clicks on a state, he or she will be taken to the matching student stack. As students explore each other's stacks, they can learn about the different states.

Planning Pages
State Brochure

Create a multimedia state brochure that includes a clickable map, an interactive timeline, and a list of fun facts that scrolls to music.

NAMES: _____

_____

STATE: _____

Directions:

Find information about your state using an encyclopedia, the Internet, or other library resources. Keep track of where you found your facts, so that you can include this information on the bibliography card of your stack.

CARD 1: COVER AND CONTENTS

Find a map of the state you chose. You can search on a CD-ROM encyclopedia or on Web sites, such as: http://www.50states.com and http://bensguide.gpo.gov/3-5/state/index.html. Save the map in your work folder as a JPG, GIF, or PICT file. Record your map source and the name of your file below.

_____

CARD 2: MAJOR CITIES

You will need information on three different cities in the state:

THE STATE'S CAPITAL: _____
What are some interesting facts about the capital?

_____

_____

ANOTHER MAJOR CITY: _____
What are some reasons that so many people live there?

_____

_____

ANOTHER MAJOR CITY: _____
Why do you think this city is interesting? What would you do there?

_____

_____

Project 6

State Brochure

CARD 3: FUN FACTS

List 3 interesting facts about the state, such as its history, natural resources, famous people born there, tourist attractions, and so on. Imagine that you're the governor and want to tell other people all the great reasons to visit this state. (If you need more space, write on the back.)

_____

_____

_____

What are some things you could draw that relate to the state? For example, for Florida you might draw a picture of an orange tree, the sun, or Disney World. You can sketch on the back of this page.

CARD 4: TIMELINE

Pick 3 significant events that happened in this state between 1700 and today. Below, write the year next to a short description of the event.

	YEAR	WHAT HAPPENED?
#1	_____	_____
#2	_____	_____
#3	_____	_____

CARD 5: BIBLIOGRAPHY

What books, articles, encyclopedias, and Internet sites did you use to research the state? Ask your teacher about what format to use for your bibliography.

_____

_____

CARD 6: ABOUT YOU

Write a short paragraph about each of you. (If you need more space, write on the back.)

_____

_____

On the Computer
State Brochure

CREATE A NEW STACK

1 Under the **FILE** menu, start a **New Stack**. Under the **EDIT** menu, click on **New Card** five times to get a total of six cards.

2 Use the **MOVE** menu to return to the **First Card**.

3 Click and drag the **TOOLS** and **COLORS** menus to either side of your card.

CARD 1: COVER AND CONTENTS

Add Clip Art of the state map for the background (see below).

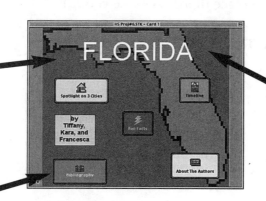

Use the **text tool** to type the title on map background (see p. 52).

Add 5 buttons that connect to other cards in the stack (see p. 52).

Add a map background:

1 Under the **FILE** menu, select **Add Clip Art**.

2 Find the state map you saved in your work folder. Open it, and use the **rectangle selector** to select the state. Click OK.

3 Enlarge the map until it fills most of the card. To do this, hold down the **shift** key as you click and drag the corner of the clip art. Then, click outside the red "marching ants."

State Brochure

Type the title:

1 Double-click on the **text tool** to select the font size and text color. Use a medium-large size, such as 48 or 72. Pick a contrasting color that will show up well against the map.

2 Type the name of your state carefully. If you make a mistake while typing, use the **delete** key to erase.

Add 5 buttons that connect to other cards in the stack:

1 Under **OBJECTS** menu, **Add a Button** that will connect to another card in the stack. Name the button "Spotlight on 3 Cities" and click OK.

2 Use the cursor to position the button on the card. (Keep in mind that you have four more buttons to place there, so make room.)

3 Click outside the button to get to the **Actions** window. Under **Places to Go**, select **Another card**. This box will appear:

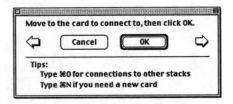

Click the right arrow to select the card you want the button to connect to. For "Spotlight on 3 Cities," select Card 2. Pick a transition, then click OK.

4 Back in the **Actions** window, under **Things to Do**, select **Play a sound** for the button. Pick a simple sound such as **Click** or **Boing**, then click OK again.

5 Repeat Steps 1–4 four times for the other buttons. Label these buttons "Fun Facts," "Timeline," "Bibliography," and "About the Authors." Connect them to Cards 3, 4, 5, and 6, respectively.

6 **Save Stack** in your work folder.

On the Computer

State Brochure

CARD 2: MAJOR CITIES

Add Clip Art of the state map. (See Card 1.)

Add a Button that connects to Card 1.

Use the **text tool** to type in instructions for the user.

Use the **text tool** to write the names of the state and the 3 cities.

Use the **paintbrush tool** to make a red dot for each of the 3 cities.

Screen labels: HS Proj#6.STK – Card 2; Tallahassee; St. Augustine; Miami; Contents; Click each of the 3 red dots to learn more about the city. Click on the dot/city again to close the text box.

Add a Text Object and Button for each city:

1 Under the **OBJECTS** menu, **Add a Text Object** next to one of the cities on your map. Use the cursor to position and change the size of the text object, if necessary. (Don't worry if it covers part of your map.)

2 Click outside the box to get to the **Text Appearance** window. Type in the city's name in the **Name** box. Choose a suitable background and text color. Then, click OK.

3 Type in the information you have about the city inside the text object.

State Brochure

4 Go back to the **OBJECTS** menu to **Add a Button**. For type of button, choose the **invisible rectangle button** (dotted rectangle). Type in the name of the city, then click OK.

5 Position and adjust the size of the button so that it surrounds the city's name and its red dot. Click outside the button to get to the **Actions** window:

   ❋ For **Places to Go**, choose **None of the Above**.

   ❋ For **Things to Do**, select **Play a sound** and pick any sound.

   ❋ Next, select **New Button Actions**. This screen will appear:

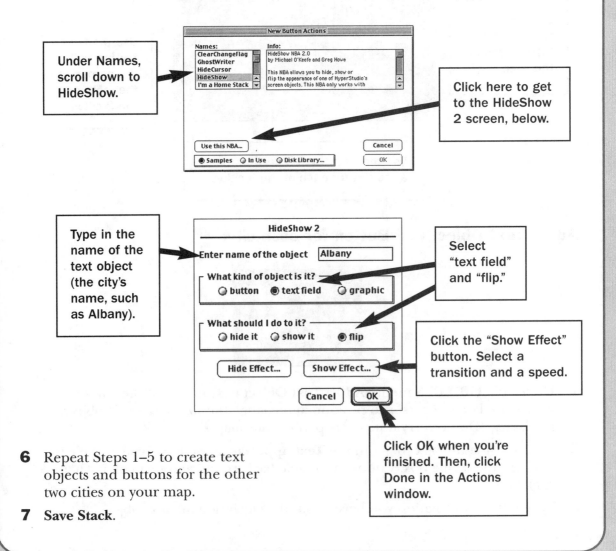

Under Names, scroll down to HideShow.

Click here to get to the HideShow 2 screen, below.

Type in the name of the text object (the city's name, such as Albany).

Select "text field" and "flip."

Click the "Show Effect" button. Select a transition and a speed.

Click OK when you're finished. Then, click Done in the Actions window.

6 Repeat Steps 1–5 to create text objects and buttons for the other two cities on your map.

7 **Save Stack**.

On the Computer
State Brochure

CARD 3: FUN FACTS

Add a non-scrolling Text Object for this card's title. (On the Text Appearance screen, remove the check marks on Draw scroll bar and Scrollable.)

Add a Button that connects to Card 1.

HS Proj#6.STK – Card 3

Fun Facts about FLORIDA

Contents

"Click" on the Florida Alligator to learn about some Cool Fun Facts about Florida.

Use **clip art** and **paint tools** to add pictures of buildings, symbols, or other objects that represent the state.

Add a Button with RollCredits feature (see p. 56).

Add a Text Object for the Fun Facts (see below).

Add a Text Object for the fun facts:

1 **Add a Text Object** and position it under your art. Adjust the size of the box.

2 Click outside the box to get to the **Text Appearance** window. Click **Draw scroll bar** to remove the check mark. Name the text object "Fun Facts."

3 Using ALL CAPS, type in instructions telling the user which object to click to see the fun facts. Below these instructions, type in your list of fun facts about the state.

TO SEE SOME COOL FACTS ABOUT FLODIA

*The first people to live in Flordia

TIP: Since this text object does not have a scroll bar, use the arrow keys on the keyboard to scroll up or down.

State Brochure

Add a Button with RollCredits feature:

1 **Add a Button** and choose the **invisible rectangle button**. Click OK.

2 Put the button around the picture that you want users to click on to read the fun facts. (See the text object, above.) For example, if you wrote, "Click on the Empire State Building to see some cool facts about NY," put the invisible button around the picture of the Empire State Building.

3 Click outside the box to get to the **Actions** window:

* For **Places to Go**, choose **None of the Above**.

* For **Things to Do**, select **Play a sound**. Pick one of the longer music sounds to play while the fun facts scroll.

* Next, click on **New Button Actions**. On the **New Button Actions** window, scroll down to **RollCredits**, and click **Use this NBA**. The **Roll Credits** window will appear:

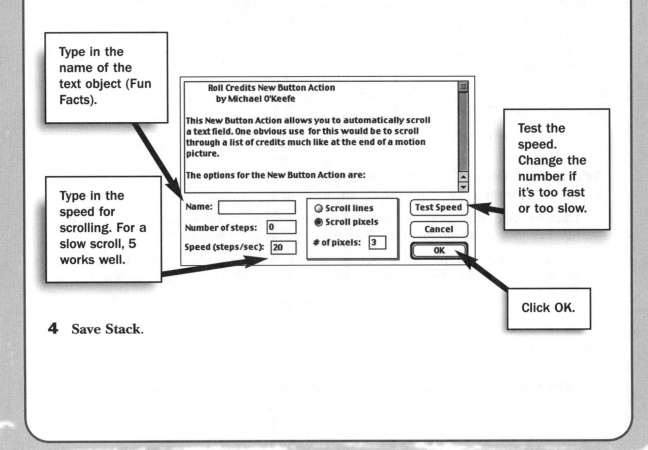

Type in the name of the text object (Fun Facts).

Type in the speed for scrolling. For a slow scroll, 5 works well.

Test the speed. Change the number if it's too fast or too slow.

Click OK.

Roll Credits New Button Action
by Michael O'Keefe

This New Button Action allows you to automatically scroll a text field. One obvious use for this would be to scroll through a list of credits much like at the end of a motion picture.

The options for the New Button Action are:

Name: [   ]
Number of steps: [0]
Speed (steps/sec): [20]

○ Scroll lines
● Scroll pixels
# of pixels: [3]

Test Speed
Cancel
OK

4 Save Stack.

On the Computer

State Brochure

CARD 4: TIMELINE

Add a non-scrolling Text Object for the card's title.

Use the **line tool** to draw a thick horizontal line across the screen. Hold down the **shift** key as you draw to get a straight line. Add 4 vertical lines, spaced evenly apart, for the years.

Add a Button that connects to Card 1.

Add 3 red-arrow icons to indicate the years in your timeline. (see the **Icon Library—Clip Art** under the **HS Art** folder.)

Use the **text tool** to type in the years and instructions.

Add 3 buttons with HideShow feature (see p. 54).

Add 3 Text Objects for the timeline facts (see below).

TIMELINE
Some Important Dates in Florida's History

contents

Hey, click the red arrow

1940   1960   1980   2000

Add 3 Text Objects for the timeline facts:

1 **Add a Text Object** below the first red arrow. Size it down so that it fits in the card.

2 On the **Text Appearance** window, click **Draw scroll bar** and **Scrollable** to remove the check marks. For **Name**, type in the **year** that the text box is about.

3 Type in the year and describe the significant event that happened in that year.

4 Repeat Steps 1–3 for the second and third arrows.

5 **Save Stack**.

On the Computer
State Brochure

CARD 5: BIBLIOGRAPHY

1 Add a <u>non-scrolling</u> **Text Object** for the title of this card.

2 Add a <u>scrolling</u> **Text Object** for the bibliography. (Leave the check marks on **Draw scroll bar** and **Scrollable**.) Type in all the resources you used to create this stack.

3 **Add a Button** that connects to Card 1.

4 **Save Stack.**

CARD 6: ABOUT THE AUTHORS

Repeat the steps in Card 5 to create Card 6. Add a picture of each author of this stack. (You can scan in a photograph, then **Add a Graphic Object** under the **OBJECTS** menu to select it. Or, you can draw a self-portrait using the paint tools.)

Check Spelling
Under the **Extras** menu, click on **Check Spelling**. Select **This stack** to check all the cards at the same time. Then, **Save Stack**.

Note:
Before you present this stack to someone, make sure that all text objects on Cards 2 and 4 are hidden. If a text object is visible, click on its button to hide it.

TIP FOR IMPROVING THIS STACK

You can attach pre-made animation to each button on the Contents card. Go to Card 1 and click the **arrow edit tool**. Double-click on the first button you want to change. On the **Button Appearance** window, click the **Actions** button. Under **Things to Do**, click **Play Animation**. Click on **Disk Library** to get the animation. In the **HS Animation** folder, choose an animation file, such as **Addycar.gif**, and click **Open**. To create the animated object's movement, hold down the mouse button and drag the object across the screen. Release the mouse button when you're done. On the **Animation** window, click on **Try it** to see how your animation looks. Click **OK**, then click **Done** on the **Actions** window.

For the Teacher

Early Explorer Report

After doing research about an early explorer of North America, students write and design a *HyperStudio* report that includes a short biography and an animated map of the explorer's route.

Before Class:

* Make a sample Early Explorer Report stack in *HyperStudio* to familiarize yourself with the steps and possible pitfalls. Your stack can serve as a model for students, as well as motivate them to complete their own.

* For each student, photocopy the Planning Pages and On the Computer instructions for this project (pages 60–68).

* Gather some library books and encyclopedia entries about early explorers of North America, such as Lewis and Clark and Sacajawea, Henry Hudson, Leif Eriksson, Juan Ponce de León, Hernando de Soto, Christopher Columbus, and Giovanni da Verrazzano. In addition, bookmark the Web sites listed on the Planning Pages, as well as other sites where students can find information on other explorers.

During Class:

* On a large map or globe, ask a student to point out North America. Explain to students that over the past 500 years, many brave people have explored this continent. Invite students to brainstorm some explorers, such as Christopher Columbus and Lewis and Clark aided by Sacajawea. Remind the class that native peoples have lived in North America for thousands of years.

* Explain to students that they will work in pairs or small groups to research an explorer. Each team will select a different explorer, then present their findings in a *HyperStudio* stack. Show the sample stack you created. Discuss the purpose of each section.

* Distribute the Planning Pages and On the Computer instructions to each student. Once you have approved a team's Planning Pages, students can design their stack on the computer.

Project 7

Early Explorer Report

Get ready to explore an explorer! After doing research on an early explorer of North America, your team will create a *HyperStudio* report that includes a brief biography and an animated map of the explorer's route.

NAMES: _____   _____

Directions:

Read a short article about this explorer's life in an encyclopedia. Then read at least two other sources to learn more about this person. Here are a couple of Web sites to start with:

Internet Sites:

http://www.win.tue.nl/~engels/discovery

http://www.bham.wednet.edu/land.htm

Explorer's Name: _____

CARD 1: COVER AND CONTENTS

Title of your stack: _____

Find a picture of the explorer on the Internet or an encyclopedia CD-ROM. Save the image in your work folder as a JPG, GIF, or PICT file. Record the file's name and its source below:

_____

CARD 2: WHO WAS HE OR SHE?

Write a paragraph explaining why this explorer is famous. When did the explorer live? What part of the world did he or she explore? What was this explorer hoping to find?

_____

_____

_____

_____

Planning Pages
Early Explorer Report

CARD 3: ANIMATED MAP

Use the Internet, books, or an encyclopedia CD-ROM to find a picture of an old map from the time when your explorer lived. Save it in your work folder as a JPG, GIF, or PICT file. (If the map comes from a book, scan it to create a computer file.) Record the file's name and its source below.

_____

Research one route that the explorer took. Draw this route on a map on the back of this page.

CARD 4: TRIUMPHS AND DISASTERS

Research some of the explorer's successes and failures. Write about two examples of each below. (If you need more space, use the back of this page.)

Triumphs _____

_____

Disasters _____

_____

CARD 5: BIBLIOGRAPHY

List all Web sites, encyclopedias, books, and other resources you used to learn about this explorer. Ask your teacher about what format to use for your bibliography.

_____

_____

CARD 6: ABOUT THE AUTHORS

Write a short paragraph about each of you.

_____

_____

_____

_____

Project 7

On the Computer
Early Explorer Report

START A NEW STACK

1 Under the **FILE** menu, start a **New Stack**. Under the **EDIT** menu, click on **New Card** five times to get a total of six cards.

2 Use the **MOVE** menu to return to the **First Card**.

3 Click and drag the **TOOLS** and **COLORS** menus to the either side of the card.

CARD 1: COVER AND CONTENTS

After you fill in the background, use the **text tool** to type the title.

Use the **paint bucket tool** to fill in the background.

> **HS Proj#7.STK – Card 1**
> Lewis & Clark
> Famous American Explorers
> Don't Forget Sacajawea
>
> ? Who Were They?
> Triumphs & Disasters
> Bibliography
> About The Authors
> Animated Map
> by Jack, Michael and Logan

Add a Graphic **Object** of your explorer (see p. 63).

Use the **rectangle tool** to draw a border. You may choose a pattern instead of a solid color.

Add 5 Buttons that connect to other cards in this stack (see p. 63).

On the Computer

Early Explorer Report

Add a Graphic Object of the explorer's picture:

1 Under the **OBJECTS** menu, select **Add a Graphic Object**. Select your work folder (where you saved your explorer's image), and double-click on the person's image file. Use the **rectangle selector** to choose the part of the picture you want to use, then click OK.

2 Click and drag the picture to one side of the card. Click outside the picture, then click OK on the **Graphic Appearance** window. To resize the picture, click on the **arrow edit tool** in the **TOOLS** box, then click on the picture. When the red "marching ants" surround the picture, hold down the **shift** key and click and drag the corner of the graphic object.

Add 5 Buttons that connect to other cards in the stack:

1 Under the **OBJECTS** menu, click **Add a Button**. Name the button "Who was he (or she)?" Then, click OK.

2 Use the cursor to position the button under the explorer's picture on the card. Keep in mind that you have four more buttons to place there, so make sure you have enough room.

3 Click outside the button to get to the **Actions** window. Under **Places to Go**, select **Another card**. This box will appear:

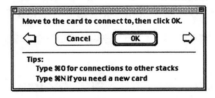

Click the **right arrow** to select the card you want the button to connect to. For "Who was he (or she)?" select Card 2. Pick a transition, then click OK.

4 Back at the **Actions** window, under **Things to Do**, select **Play a sound**. Pick a simple sound, then click OK. Click **Done**.

5 Repeat Steps 1–4 four times for the other buttons. Label these buttons "Animated Map," "Triumphs and Disasters," "Bibliography," and "About the Authors." Connect the buttons to Cards 3, 4, 5, and 6, respectively.

6 **Save Stack** in your work folder.

On the Computer
Early Explorer Report

CARD 2: WHO WAS HE (OR SHE)?

Add a Text Object for the card title (see below).

Add a Graphic Object of a picture of the explorer.

Add a Text Object for your short biography of the explorer (see below).

HS Proj#7.STK – Card 2

Who Were Lewis, Clark & Sacajawea?

Meriwether Lewis and William Clark, better known as Lewis and Clark, were famous explorers. They were asked by President Thomas Jefferson to find a way to travel from the Atlantic Ocean to the Pacific Ocean using water. They started looking for it in 1804 and returned in 1806. During that time they traveled over 8,000 miles. 48 men were part

Home Page   Next Page

Add a Button that connects to the next card.

Add a Button that connects to the cover card. On the Actions screen, select Another card under Places to Go, and connect this button to Card 1.

Add a Text Object for the card title and biography:

1 Under the **OBJECTS** menu, select **Add a Text Object**. A rectangular box with red "marching ants" will appear. Click inside the box and drag it near the top of the card. Move the cursor to any side of the box to resize it. Then, click outside the box.

2 In the **Text Appearance** window, click on **Style** and choose a font and large font size, as well as text and background colors for the text object. Click OK.

3 Back at the **Text Appearance** screen, click on **Draw scroll bar** and **Scrollable** to remove the check marks. Click OK again.

On the Computer

Early Explorer Report

4 Type in the card's title.

5 Repeat Steps 1–3 to **Add a Text Object** for your biography. Position the text object under your title. This time, use a smaller font size and leave the check marks on **Draw scroll bar** and **Scrollable**. Type in your explorer's biography.

Copy and Paste Buttons to other cards:

Cards 2, 3, 4, and 5 all need two buttons: one that goes to the next card, and another that goes to Card 1. (Card 6 needs only a button that goes to Card 1.) Instead of making these buttons from scratch, you can copy and paste the two buttons you created on Card 2. Here's how:

1 Click on the **arrow edit tool**, then click on the "next card" button. Red "marching ants" will appear around the button. Go to the **EDIT** menu and select **Copy button**.

2 Under the **MOVE** menu, click on **Next Card**. Then, go back to the **EDIT** menu and select **Paste button**.

3 Repeat Steps 1–2 for Cards 4 and 5.

4 Use the **MOVE** menu to **Jump to Card** 2. Repeat Steps 1–3 with the other button (the one that connects to Card 1) for Cards 3 to 6.

5 **Save Stack** in your work folder.

CARD 3: ANIMATED MAP

Add a non-scrolling Text Object for the title. (On the Text Appearance window, remove the check marks from Draw scroll bar and Scrollable.)

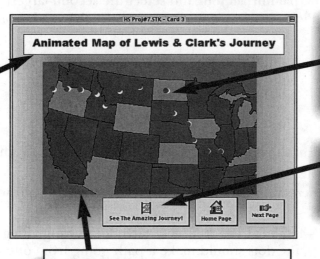

Create an animation that shows the explorer's route (see p. 66).

Add a Button that plays animation (see p. 67).

Add Clip Art of a map (see p. 66).

Early Explorer Report

Add Clip Art of a map and reduce its brightness:

1 Under the **FILE** menu, select **Add Clip Art**.

2 Open your work folder and click on the old map you used in Card 2. Open it, and use the **rectangle selector** to surround the part of the map you want to use. Click OK.

3 Use the corner arrows to enlarge the map until it fills the center of the card. **Tip:** Hold down the **shift** key as you click and drag the corner, so that the clip art will enlarge evenly.

4 While the map is still surrounded by red "marching ants," go to the **EDIT** menu and choose **Effects**. Select *HyperStudio* **Effects**, then choose **Brightness/Contrast**.

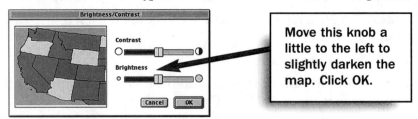

Move this knob a little to the left to slightly darken the map. Click OK.

Create an animation showing the explorer's route:

1 Under the **FILE** menu, select **Export Screen**. Save the image <u>in your work folder</u> as **New.Pic.01** (or **Pict1** in Windows).

2 Double-click the **paintbrush tool** and select the second-largest circle size, and click OK. Pick a bright, contrasting color, such as red, from the **COLORS** box.

3 Use the **paintbrush tool** to make a single dot on the map, at the starting point of the explorer's journey.

4 Select **Export Screen** again and save the revised map in your work folder as **New.Pic.02**.

5 Repeat Steps 3–4 about 15 to 20 times, each dot moving along the explorer's route. Together, the dots should make a path going from one end of the explorer's route to the other.

6 **Save Stack**.

Early Explorer Report

Add a Button that plays the animation:

1 **Add a Button** with an icon and label that says something like, "See the explorer's journey!" Place the button below the map.

2 On the **Actions** window, select **None of the Above** under **Places to Go**. Choose **Play a sound** under **Things to Do**. On the **Tape Deck** screen, select **Disk Library** and select a short piece of music. Then, click OK.

3 Back in the **Actions** window, click on **Play animation** under **Things to Do**. Click on **Disk Library** to get the animation, and go to your work folder. Find the **New.Pic.01** (or **Pict1**) file and click it. Use the **rectangle selector** to select the area directly around the map, then click OK.

4 Wait while *HyperStudio* combines all the **New.Pic** files and creates an animation file. A second copy of the map will appear over your original version. Use the mouse to move the second copy of the map exactly on top of the original. Then click the mouse. The **Animation** window will appear:

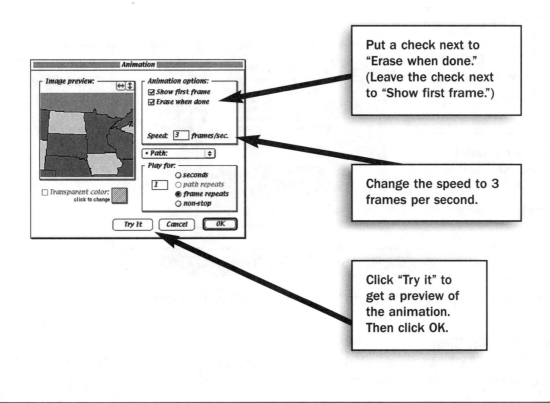

Put a check next to "Erase when done." (Leave the check next to "Show first frame.")

Change the speed to 3 frames per second.

Click "Try it" to get a preview of the animation. Then click OK.

On the Computer

Early Explorer Report

CARD 4: TRIUMPHS AND DISASTERS

Add a non-scrolling Text Object for the title.

Use the **paint bucket tool** to fill the background with color.

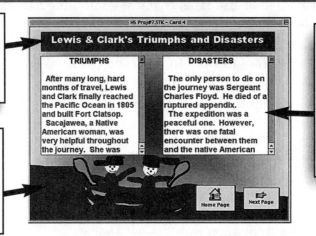

Add 2 scrolling Text Objects — one for triumphs and one for disasters. (Leave the check marks on Draw scroll bar and Scrollable.)

CARD 5: BIBLIOGRAPHY

Add a non-scrolling Text Object for the title.

Use the **paint bucket tool** to fill in the background.

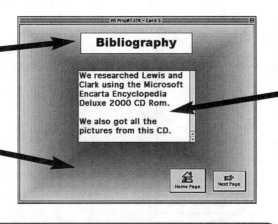

Add a scrolling Text Object for the bibliography.

CARD 6: ABOUT THE AUTHORS

Repeat the steps in Card 5. Add a picture of each author of this stack.

Check Spelling

Under the **EXTRAS** menu, click on **Check Spelling**. Select **This stack** to check all the cards at once. Then, **Save Stack**.

For the Teacher

Space Exploration Timeline

During the last century, we made remarkable progress exploring the moon, the planets, and the universe beyond. In this project, students pick a theme in space exploration, research four milestones, and then present their findings in an interactive timeline.

Before Class:

✳ Make a sample Space Exploration Timeline stack to familiarize yourself with the procedure and possible pitfalls. Your stack will motivate students and provide a model for them.

✳ For each student, photocopy the Planning Pages and On the Computer instructions for this project (pages 70–78).

✳ Gather some books from your library about famous space missions, such as Apollo, Viking, Voyager, and Pathfinder. Bookmark the astronomy Web sites listed on the Planning Pages, so students can access them easily.

During Class:

✳ Ask students: What is a timeline? *(A diagram that tracks the history of important events in the order in which they happened.)* Have students brainstorm a list of possible themes or topics for a space timeline. Let them browse through books to help spark ideas.

✳ Tell students that they will work in pairs (or small groups) to make a *HyperStudio* timeline that presents information about four different events in space history. Show the sample stack you created. Discuss the purpose of each section of the stack.

✳ Explain that each group will create a timeline about a different theme, such as Apollo moon missions, famous firsts, Mars exploration, women in space, unpiloted missions, space-exploration tragedies, or the Hubble Space Telescope.

✳ Point out some resources that can help students in their research: NASA Web sites, encyclopedias, and reference books such as *Amazing Space: A Book of Answers for Kids* by Ann-Jeanette Campbell (The New York Public Library).

✳ Distribute copies of the Planning Pages and On the Computer instructions to each student. Once you have approved a team's Planning Pages, students can design their stack on the computer.

Project 8

Planning Pages
Space Exploration Timeline

Over the past 50 years, humans have made amazing progress exploring space. In this project, you and a partner will pick a theme in space exploration, research four milestones, then present your findings in an interactive timeline.

NAMES: _____   _____

Directions:

Choose a theme you would like to concentrate on for your space-exploration timeline. For example, the Apollo moon missions, women in space, unmanned space probes, or space stations. Research your topic in encyclopedias, books, the Internet, or other library resources.

Internet Sites:

http://spacekids.hq.nasa.gov/

http://antwrp.gsfc.nasa.gov/apod

http://www.space.com/spacelinks/

CARD 1: COVER

Title for your stack:

_____

Find a space photo to use for a background. You can either scan a picture or download an image from the Internet or a CD-ROM. Make a folder called "Space Photos" in your work folder, and save the space photo in this folder as a JPG, GIF, or PICT file. Record the source of your image and the image's file name below:

_____

Write a short introduction to record on the computer. Introduce the topic of your timeline and explain why you chose it. Then, tell readers what part of the background they should click to go on. For example: "Welcome to Ben and Quincy's space exploration stack. We did our project on the Apollo missions to the moon because we'd like to be astronauts. To see a timeline of space milestones, click the picture of the Earth." (If you need more space, write on the back.)

_____

Planning Pages
Space Exploration Timeline

CARDS 2–6: TIMELINE

Collect space photos related to your timeline. In addition to the Web sites listed on p. 70, you can find some space photographs in *HyperStudio*'s **Media Library**. Go to the **Photo Gallery** and open the **Space** folder to see them. Keep track of where you found your facts, so that you can include this information on the bibliography card of your stack. Save the space images you collected in your "Space Photos" folder (in your work folder) as a JPG, GIF, or PICT file.

Fill in the chart on the next page with information about each of the four events in your timeline. Record the date of the event, a paragraph detailing what happened, and your source for a photo of this event. As you write the paragraph for each timeline event, here are some questions to keep in mind:

* What makes this mission important in the history of space exploration?
* What questions did astronomers want to answer? What kinds of information did scientists learn?
* Who were some of the scientists or astronauts involved in this mission?

DATE	WHAT HAPPENED?	PICTURE
July 20, 1969	Astronaut Neil Armstrong walked on the Moon. He said, "That's one small step for a man, one giant leap for mankind." Most of the huge TV audience did not hear Armstrong say the word "a" before "man" because of a gap in the transmission.	World Book Encyclopedia CD, article on Neil Armstrong.

CARD 7: BIBLIOGRAPHY

What books, articles, encyclopedias and Internet sites did you use for your research? Ask your teacher about what format to use for your bibliography.

_____

_____

CARD 8: ABOUT THE AUTHORS

Write a short paragraph about each of you. (If you need more space, write on the back.)

_____

_____

_____

Planning Pages
Space Exploration Timeline

DATE	WHAT HAPPENED?	PICTURE
Event 1 (Card 3)		
Event 2 (Card 4)		
Event 3 (Card 5)		
Event 4 (Card 6)		

On the Computer
Space Exploration Timeline

START A NEW STACK

1 Under the **FILE** menu, start a **New Stack**. Under the **EDIT** menu, click on **New Card** seven times to get a total of eight cards.

2 Use the **MOVE** menu to return to the **First Card**.

3 Click and drag the **TOOLS** and **COLORS** menus to either side of the card.

CARD 1: COVER

Under the **FILE** menu, select **Import Background**. Choose a space photo from your work folder.

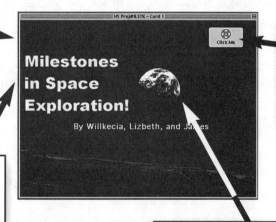

Add a Button that plays a recording of your introduction (see below).

Use the **text tool** to type the title of your stack on the card. Use a fun font in a large size.

Add a Button (invisible) that connects to Card 2 (see p. 74).

Add a Button with a recording of your voice:

1 From the **OBJECTS** menu, select **Add a Button**. When the **Button Appearance** window pops up, click on the **Icons** button. Select **Disk Library** on the **Icons** window. Under the **HS Art** folder, click **Icon Library**. Select an icon that indicates sound, such as a microphone, a stereo speaker, or an ear. Then, click OK.

2 Name the button something like "Click me" or "Welcome." Click OK.

3 On the card, you'll see the button with red "marching ants" around it. Place the cursor inside this button and click and drag it to one corner of the card. Then click outside the button.

On the Computer

Space Exploration Timeline

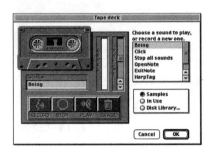

4 When the **Actions** window appears, select **None of the Above** for **Places to Go**. Pick **Play a sound** under **Things to Do**. When the **Tape Deck** screen appears, click **Record**. Read your introduction into the computer's microphone, then click **Stop**. Click **Play** to check your recording. Then click OK.

Add an Invisible Button:

1 From the **OBJECTS** menu, select **Add a Button**. Pick the **invisible rectangle button**, and click OK.

2 Click and drag the button so that it surrounds the part of the background you want the reader to click. Then, click outside the button.

3 On the **Actions** window, select **Next card** for **Places to Go**, and pick a transition. For **Things to Do**, select **Play a sound** and pick a simple sound. Click **Done**.

4 **Save Stack** in your work folder.

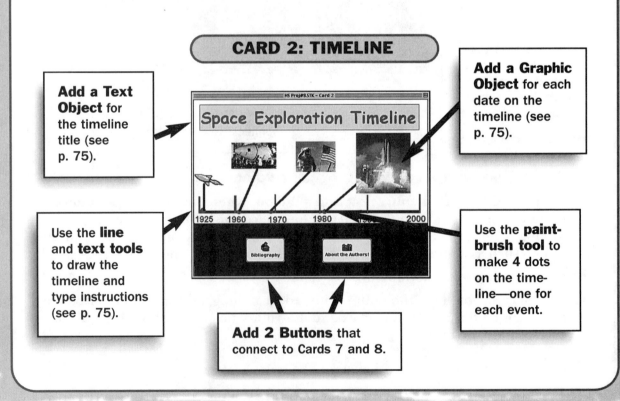

CARD 2: TIMELINE

Add a Text Object for the timeline title (see p. 75).

Add a Graphic Object for each date on the timeline (see p. 75).

Space Exploration Timeline

1925　1960　1970　1980　　2000

Use the **line** and **text tools** to draw the timeline and type instructions (see p. 75).

Use the **paint-brush tool** to make 4 dots on the time-line—one for each event.

Add 2 Buttons that connect to Cards 7 and 8.

On the Computer
Space Exploration Timeline

Add a Text Object for the title:

1 Under the **OBJECTS** menu, select **Add a Text Object**. A rectangular box with red "marching ants" will appear. Click inside the box and drag it near the top of the card. Move the cursor to any side of the box to resize it. Then, click outside the box.

2 In the **Text Appearance** window, click on **Style** and choose a font and large font size, as well as text and background colors for the text object. Click OK.

3 Back at the **Text Appearance** window, click on **Draw scroll bar** and **Scrollable** to remove the check marks. Click OK again.

4 Type in your title in the text object.

Draw the timeline and type instructions:

1 Double-click on the **line tool** and select a thick line to draw the timeline. Click OK.

2 While holding down the **shift** key, draw a thick horizontal line across the screen. Then use the **line tool** to add evenly spaced vertical lines along the timeline.

3 Use the **text tool** to type in the years and instructions to the reader. Instruct readers to click on a picture above the timeline to learn more about an event.

Add 4 Graphic Objects above the timeline:

1 From the **OBJECTS** menu, select **Add a Graphic Object**. In your work folder, find the image file you saved earlier that goes with the earliest event on your timeline. Use the **rectangle selector** to surround the photo. Click OK.

2 The graphic object appears on Card 2 with red "marching ants" around it. Click and drag the image to a place near the dot that goes with it. Then click outside the object.

3 On the **Graphic Appearance** window, click the **Actions** button. For **Places to Go**, select **Another card**. This box will appear:

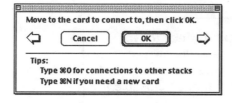

On the Computer

Space Exploration Timeline

4 Click the right arrow until you get to the card you want the button to connect to. For the first timeline event, select Card 3. Pick a transition, then click OK.

5 Back at the **Actions** window, select **Play a sound** under **Things to Do**. Pick a sound, then click OK. Click **Done**.

6 If you want to make the graphic object smaller, click the **arrow edit tool**, then click on the object. Hold down the **shift** key, and click and drag the corner arrows to make the object smaller.

7 Use the **line tool** to draw a thin line connecting the graphic object with the painted dot that goes with it.

8 Repeat Steps 1–7 three times to create other graphic objects for your timeline. Connect the second timeline event (graphic object) to Card 4, the third one to Card 5, and the fourth one to Card 6.

(**CARDS 3–6: EVENT CARDS**)

Repeat the same steps for Cards 3 through 6.

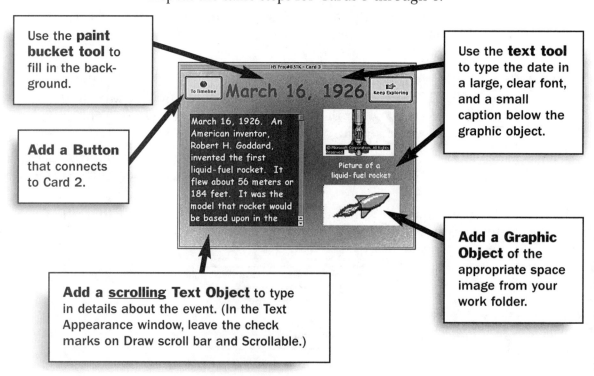

Use the **paint bucket tool** to fill in the background.

Add a **Button** that connects to Card 2.

Add a **scrolling** Text Object to type in details about the event. (In the Text Appearance window, leave the check marks on Draw scroll bar and Scrollable.)

Use the **text tool** to type the date in a large, clear font, and a small caption below the graphic object.

Add a **Graphic Object** of the appropriate space image from your work folder.

March 16, 1926. An American inventor, Robert H. Goddard, invented the first liquid-fuel rocket. It flew about 56 meters or 184 feet. It was the model that rocket would be based upon in the

March 16, 1926

Picture of a liquid-fuel rocket

On the Computer
Space Exploration Timeline

CARD 7: BIBLIOGRAPHY

Add a non-scrolling Text Object for the title. (Remove the check marks for Draw scroll bar and Scrollable.)

Add a Button that connects to Card 2.

Add a scrolling Text Object for the bibliography.

CARD 8: ABOUT THE AUTHORS

Repeat the steps in Card 7 to make Card 8. Add a picture of each author of this stack.

Check Spelling

Under the **EXTRAS** menu, click on **Check Spelling**. Select **This stack** to check all the cards at once. Then, **Save Stack**.

On the Computer

Space Exploration Timeline

TIP FOR IMPROVING THIS STACK

The Mac version of *HyperStudio* and the Windows version of *HyperStudio* 4.0 have an interesting feature called "Blabbermouth II," which reads text objects aloud. You can add this feature to your timeline events cards:

Give this scrolling Text Object a name (see below).

Add a Button with Blabbermouth feature (see below).

1 From the **MOVE** menu, **Jump to Card** 3, the first event on your timeline. Click the **arrow edit tool**, then double-click the text object describing the event. Give this text object a one-word name that has to do with the event. Jot the name on a piece of paper—you'll need it soon.

2 **Add a Button** and choose an icon that indicates sound, such as an ear (click on the **Disk Library** and choose **Icon Library** in the **HS Art** folder).

3 Position the button in one corner and click outside it. On the **Actions** window, select **None of the Above** for **Places to Go**. Under **Things to Do**, select **New Button Actions**.

4 On the **New Buttons** window, select **Blabbermouth II**, then click **Use this NBA**. A choice screen will appear. In the box below **Text or name of text field to read**, type in the name of your text object. Select a rate, pitch, and voice. Click on the **Try it** button to experiment with different sound combinations. Once you're happy with the way the computer reads your words, click OK.

5 Repeat Steps 1–4 for Cards 4–6. Make sure you give each text object a different name.

Math Story and Quiz

Students write a humorous short story in which a character uses math to solve problems. Multiple-choice quizzes are woven into the plot of the story.

Before Class:

✳ Make a sample Math Story and Quiz stack in *HyperStudio* to familiarize yourself with the procedure and possible pitfalls. This stack will motivate students and provide a model for them.

✳ For each student, photocopy the Planning Pages and On the Computer instructions for this project (pages 80–86).

During Class:

✳ Explain to students that they will work in pairs to create a funny story that contains math problems. Ask students to brainstorm a list of situations in which people might use math to solve problems in their lives. For example, visiting the supermarket, estimating how long it will take to travel to a certain destination, making a meal for a large number of people, or reading a train schedule.

✳ Show students the sample stack that you prepared earlier. Let students click their way through the screens and try the quiz questions.

✳ Explain that for this project, students may want to create backgrounds using the **Photo Gallery** in *HyperStudio's* **Media Library**. Show students how to get to the **Photo Gallery**, and open a few of the photo folders to show some of the photos available. These photos might give students ideas for their stories.

✳ Distribute the Planning Pages and instructions to each student. Once you have approved a team's Planning Pages, students can design their stack on the computer.

Project 9

Planning Pages
Math Story and Quiz

**In this project, you'll create a funny math story in *HyperStudio*.
To get to the end of your story, the reader will have to correctly answer
several quiz questions that you make up.**

NAMES: _____   _____

CARD 1: COVER

Story Title: _____
       (**TIP:** You may find it easier to write the title after you write the story.)

CARD 2: INTRODUCE THE MAIN CHARACTER

Invent a name for your main character—the funnier, the better.

_____

Sketch a picture of this character on the back of the page.

What does this character enjoy doing?

_____

What is something that this character dislikes?

_____

What is something that this character really wants? Why?

_____

Planning Pages
Math Story and Quiz

Write a short introduction (about 2–3 sentences) in which the character tells the reader what he or she loves and wants. (See the example in the On the Computer instructions.)

_____

_____

_____

CARD 3: INTRODUCE THE STORY PROBLEM

What are some obstacles that could get in the way of this character's goal?

_____

_____

What are some ways in which this character might use math to overcome these obstacles?

_____

_____

In 2–3 sentences, have the character tell the reader about one of these obstacles.

_____

_____

_____

CARD 4: FIRST MATH PROBLEM

Write the next part of the story. Explain how this character will try to solve the problem by using math. In the last line, ask a question. Then list three possible answers to that question—one correct and two wrong answers. Circle the correct answer.

_____

_____

_____

_____

Project 9

Math Story and Quiz

ANSWER A _____

ANSWER B _____

ANSWER C _____

CARD 5: SECOND MATH PROBLEM

Write the next part of the story. Add a new obstacle that prevents the character from getting what he or she wants. Suggest a solution that involves math. In the last line, ask a question. Then list three possible answers to that question—one correct and two wrong answers. Circle the correct answer.

_____

_____

ANSWER A _____

ANSWER B _____

ANSWER C _____

CARD 6: THIRD MATH PROBLEM

Write the next part of the story. Add another obstacle that gets in the way of the character's goal. Suggest a solution that involves math. In the last line, ask a question. Then list three possible answers to that question—one correct and two wrong answers. Circle the correct answer.

_____

_____

ANSWER A _____

ANSWER B _____

ANSWER C _____

CARD 7: ABOUT THE AUTHORS

Write a short paragraph about each of you.

_____

_____

_____

On the Computer
Math Story and Quiz

START A NEW STACK

1 Under the **FILE** menu, start a **New Stack**. Under the **EDIT** menu, click on **New Card** five times to get a total of six cards.

2 Use the **MOVE** menu to return to the **First Card**.

3 Click and drag the **TOOLS** and **COLORS** menus, and place them on either side of the card.

Add background using the Gradients effect (see below).

Use the **text tool** to type your names and the title in a fun font.

Add a **Button** that connects to the next card (see below).

CARD 1: COVER

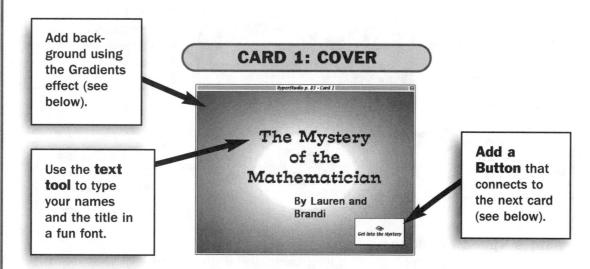

Add Background with the Gradients effect:
1 From the **EDIT** menu, select **Effects**, then choose **Gradients**.

2 When the **Gradients** screen appears, pick two contrasting colors. Choose **Vertical**, **Horizontal**, **Circular**, or **Rectangular**, then click **Apply**.

Add a Button that connects to the next card:
1 From the **OBJECTS** menu, select **Add a Button**. When the **Button Appearance** window pops up, type something like "Next" or "Let's go!" in the **Name** box.

2 Click on the **Icons** button at the bottom of the screen. Select the 👉 icon in the **Icons** window, then click OK. Click OK again on the **Button Appearance** window.

3 You'll see the button with red "marching ants" around it in the middle of the card. Click and drag the button to the right side of the card. Then click outside the button.

On the Computer

Math Story and Quiz

4 When the **Actions** window appears, select **Next card** for **Places to Go**. Pick a transition, then click OK. Back on the **Actions** window, click **Play a sound** under **Things to Do**. Select a sound, then click OK. Click **Done** in the **Actions** screen.

5 **Save Stack** in your work folder.

CARD 2: MAIN CHARACTER

Add background using the Gradients effect.

Use the **oval** and **line tools** to make a speech balloon (see below).

Use the **paint tools** to draw the main character looking happy.

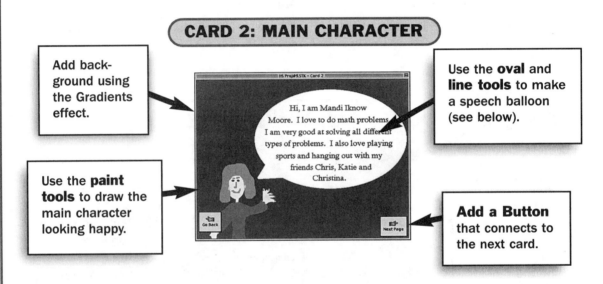

Add a Button that connects to the next card.

Create a speech balloon:

1 Before you do this step, add the background and draw a picture of your main character.

2 Double-click on the **oval tool**, then select a light color in the **COLORS** box, such as white or yellow. Click and drag the mouse to make a large oval next to the character's head.

3 Double-click on the **line tool**, and select the thickest line. Draw two short lines to make a triangle coming out of the speech balloon, pointing toward the character. Select the **paintbrush tool** to fill in the triangle.

4 Use the **text tool** to type the text inside the speech balloon. Type carefully. If you make a mistake, use the **Delete** key. Press **Return** to get to the next line. Once you click the mouse, it will be difficult to edit the text.

CARD 3: STORY PROBLEM

Repeat the steps in Card 2, except this time draw your character looking unhappy. In the speech balloon, type the character talking about a problem.

On the Computer
Math Story and Quiz

CARDS 4–6: MATH QUIZ

Add a background.

HS Proj#9.STK – Card 3

When my friends and I got to math class, we found out we were going to play "Who Wants to Be a Mathematician?" My friends were happy. I was not. Chris went to the board and got $10 for getting the answer right. Katie had to use her "friend lifeline" and she chose me! I tried to get out of helping, but the teacher called me to the board and said, "Try!" The problem was...

144 ÷ 12 = ?

Go Back

6   12   10

Add a Text Object for the math problem (see below).

Add 3 Text Objects for the multiple-choice answers to the question (see below).

Add a Text Object for the math problem:

1 Under the **OBJECTS** menu, click **Add a Text Object**. Position the rectangle near the top of the card.

2 Click outside the rectangle to get to the **Text Appearance** window. Click on **Style** and select a font and medium font size, as well as text and background colors. Click OK.

3 In the text object, type the next part of your math story and question.

Add 3 Text Objects for the quiz answers:

1 **Add a Text Object** and resize it to make a small rectangle. Move the text object to the bottom of the screen. (Keep in mind that you have to place two more text objects there, so leave room.) On the **Text Appearance** window, pick a background color. Then click **Draw scroll bar** and **Scrollable** to remove the check marks.

2 This next step will depend on whether or not the text object will have the correct answer:

✳ For the Correct Answer: On the **Text Appearance** window, click **Actions**. Select **Next Card** for **Places to Go**, and pick a transition. Under **Things to Do**, click **Play a sound**. On the **Tape Deck** screen, record your voice, congratulating the reader and explaining why the choice is correct. Click OK, then click **Done** on the **Actions** window. Type the correct answer in the text object.

✳ For the Incorrect Answers: On the **Text Appearance** window, click **Actions**. Select **None of the Above** for **Places to Go**. Under **Things to Do**, click **Play a sound**. On the **Tape Deck** window, record your voice, telling the reader to try again. Type an incorrect answer in the text object.

On the Computer
Math Story and Quiz

TIP: Vary the position of the "correct" text object on each card. Sometimes put it on the left, the middle, or the right.

CARD 7: END OF STORY

Copy Card 2 to create Card 7 (see below).

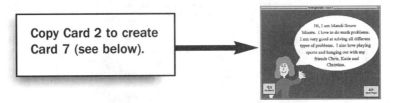

Copy Card 2 to create Card 7:

1 Under the **MOVE** menu, **Jump to Card** 2. From the **EDIT** menu, select **Copy Card**.

2 Use the **MOVE** menu to **Jump to Card** 6 (the last math problem card). Then, go to the **EDIT** menu and select **Paste Card**. A duplicate of Card 2 will appear as Card 7.

3 Use the **eraser** to erase the words in the speech balloon. Then, use the **text tool** to type in the end of your story.

CARD 8: ABOUT THE AUTHORS

Use the **text tool** to type the title.

Add a **scrolling Text Object** for your biographies.

Add a **Graphic Object** of your pictures.

Add a **Button** that connects to Card 1.

Run **Check Spelling** under the **EXTRAS** menu. Then, **Save Stack**.

For the Teacher

Class Yearbook

At the end of the school year, the whole class collaborates on a multimedia yearbook, which features a class photograph, an interactive timeline, field-trip memories, a short summary of subjects studied, and a fun quiz.

Before Class:

✳ Make a sample Class Yearbook stack in *HyperStudio* to familiarize yourself with the steps and possible pitfalls. This stack will provide students with a model, as well as motivate them to complete their own. NOTE: Once your students have completed a yearbook, it can be used as the model and motivator for future classes.

✳ For each student, photocopy the Planning Pages and On the Computer instructions for this project (pages 88–96). Since this is a collaborative project, students will find it useful to browse through all the planning pages and instructions, not just those that directly relate to their part of the stack.

✳ You will need some digitized photographs of your students for this project. You can either scan in print photos, or take pictures with a digital camera.

During Class:

✳ Explain the goal of this project: to create a multimedia class yearbook in *HyperStudio*. Unlike the other projects in this book, each group of students will work on only one part of the whole stack. Let students click through your sample class yearbook.

✳ Write the sections of this stack on the board: Cover, Table of Contents, Who's Who, Timeline, Field Trips, Subjects, and Quiz. Have 2 or 3 student create the card for each section. If you have a large class, you can assign more students to work on the timeline, field trips, or the quiz, as these sections can easily be more than one card. Students can also make up additional sections, such as Sports, Performances, a Top 10 list, and so on.

✳ Distribute the planning pages and instructions to each group. Once you have approved the Planning Pages, students can design their cards on the computer.

✳ When all the cards have been completed, use the **Copy Card** feature to combine all the cards into a single stack.

Project 10

Planning Pages
Class Yearbook

Can you believe it's almost the end of the year already? In this project, you'll collaborate with students in your class to make a multimedia yearbook in *HyperStudio*. This stack will help you summarize some of your favorite moments, and share these experiences with others.

NAMES: _____   _____

CARD 1: COVER

What title will you put on the cover?

_____

Pick a musical selection that will automatically play when the reader opens this stack. It should be about 15 seconds long. You can pick a piece of music from the *HyperStudio* CD (see page 92), play a favorite tape into the computer's microphone, or sing a song yourselves.

_____

CARD 2: TABLE OF CONTENTS

On the back of this page, sketch some pictures of things that remind you of school, such as books, a school bus, or a computer. (You will redraw these pictures on the computer for the card's background.)

CARD 3: WHO'S WHO?

Take a group photo of your class, and ask your teacher to help you turn it into a computer file, if it isn't one already. Make a list of all the students in the photograph, going one row at a time. (Use the back of this page if you need more space.)

The students in our class:

_____

_____

_____

Planning Pages
Class Yearbook

CARD 4: TIMELINE

Pick four significant events that happened in your class this year. For each one, record the month it happened, a short description of the event, and a piece of clip art or a photograph that will represent it on the timeline.

MONTH   **WHAT HAPPENED?**

_____   _____

                   Clip Art: _____

_____   _____

                   Clip Art: _____

_____   _____

                   Clip Art: _____

_____   _____

                   Clip Art: _____

CARD 5: FIELD TRIP

Pick a favorite field trip that your class went on this year. Find 1–3 photographs from this field trip. Ask your teacher to help you make the photos into computer files by scanning them. When you make this card on the computer, you will record a few memories of this field trip. Below, plan what you will talk about. (If you need more space, write on the back.)

Student's name: _____

What I Remember: _____

_____

_____

Project 10

Planning Pages

Class Yearbook

Student's name: _____

What I Remember: _____

_____

_____

CARD 6: SCHOOL SUBJECTS

Write a few sentences about some of the topics that you studied this year. Be as detailed as possible. Don't just write Language Arts. Instead, say things like, "We learned how to write plays and did an author study on Beverly Cleary."

_____

_____

_____

_____

CARD 7: QUIZ

Write a funny multiple-choice quiz about something that happened in the classroom this year. Write three possible answers (only one is correct, of course). If the reader picks the right answer, write a congratulatory message that you'll record on the computer. If the reader picks an incorrect answer, decide what you will say on the recording.

Question: _____

Answer A: _____

Answer B: _____

Answer C: _____

What will your recording say if the reader picks the correct answer?

_____

_____

What if the reader picks the wrong answers?

_____

_____

On the Computer
Class Yearbook

IMPORTANT NOTE

This stack will be built by different teams. Each team will create, write, and design one section/card of the yearbook. As you create each card, save it in your work folder. At the end, your teacher will help copy and paste all the cards into one stack.

CARD 1: COVER

Use the **paint bucket tool** to fill the background with a solid color.

Use the **text tool** to type your title in a large bold font.

Use the **Draw Multiple tool** to add "fireworks" to the background (see below).

Add a **Button** (invisible) for automatic actions (see below).

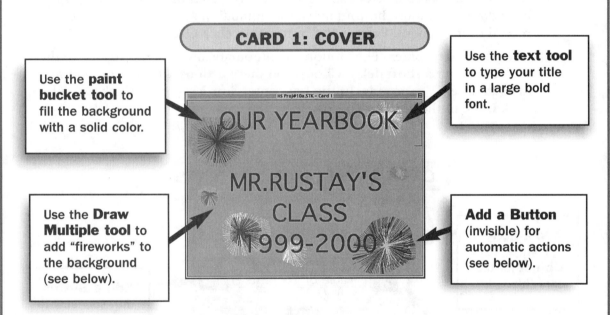

Use the Draw Multiple tool:

1 Double-click on the **line tool**, and pick the thinnest line. Click OK.

2 Select a color or pattern that will stand out against the background.

3 Go to the **OPTIONS** menu and select **Draw Multiple**. Click and hold down the mouse button and make a small circle on the background with the **line tool**. You'll create a shape that looks like fireworks. Create more fireworks in different colors. Cool, huh?

Add a Button with automatic actions:

1 From the **OBJECTS** menu, click on **Add a Button**. Under **Type**, select the **invisible rectangle button**. Click OK, then click and drag the button to one corner of the card.

2 Click outside the button to get to the **Actions** window. Under **Places to Go**, choose **Next Card**. Pick a transition, then click OK.

Class Yearbook

3 For **Things to Do**, select these three choices:

* Click **Play a sound**. On the **Tape Deck** window, you can either record your own music (about 15 seconds long) –OR– you can click **Disk Library** and open the **Sounds & Music** folder (on the CD), and select **Musical**. Pick any sound you like, then click OK.

* Click **Play animation**. Select any fun animation from the **Disk Library**. As you hold down the mouse button, move the animation across the screen to record its movement. Release the button and click OK.

* Click **Automatic timer**. This option will automatically take the reader to the next card after a short delay. Choose **Do these actions after card is shown. Activate after ___ seconds**. In the box, enter 4 or 5 seconds. Click OK. Then, click **Done** in the **Actions** window.

4 **Save Stack**.

CARD 2: TABLE OF CONTENTS

Add a **non-scrolling Text Object** for the card title.

Add a **Button** that connects to the next card.

Add a **Button** that connects to the previous card.

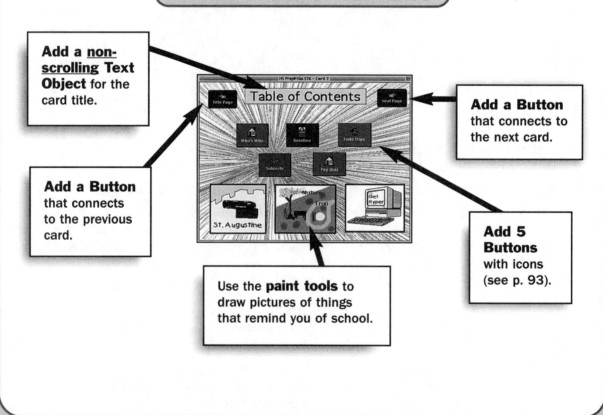

Add **5 Buttons** with icons (see p. 93).

Use the **paint tools** to draw pictures of things that remind you of school.

On the Computer
Class Yearbook

Add 5 Buttons with icons:

1 **Add a Button** and name it "Who's Who." Click on the **Icons** button and select an icon to go with your button. Then, click OK.

2 Position the button in the card. Keep in mind that you have to add four more buttons, so make room.

3 Click outside the button to get to the **Actions** window. For **Things to Do**, choose **Play a sound**, and select any sound. For now, don't check anything under **Places to Go**. (Later, when all the cards in the stack are finished and have been copied into the same stack, use the **arrow edit tool** to connect the five buttons to their respective cards.)

4 Repeat Steps 1–3 to add the other buttons. Name the buttons "Timeline," "Field Trips," "Subjects," and "Pop Quiz."

5 **Save Stack**.

CARD 3: WHO'S WHO?

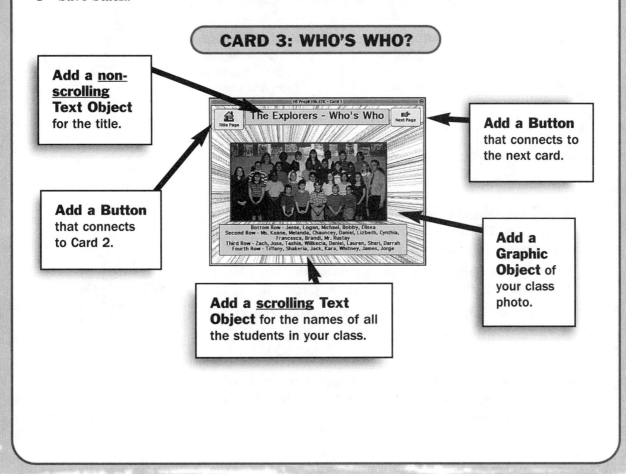

Add a <u>non-scrolling</u> **Text Object** for the title.

Add a **Button** that connects to Card 2.

Add a **Button** that connects to the next card.

Add a **Graphic Object** of your class photo.

Add a <u>scrolling</u> **Text Object** for the names of all the students in your class.

On the Computer

Class Yearbook

CARD 4: TIMELINE

Add a Button that connects to Card 2.

Add a non-scrolling Text Object for the card title.

Add a Button that connects to the next card.

Add Clip Art for each of the 4 events.

Holding down the **shift** key, use the **line tool** to draw the timeline.

The Explorers - Timeline

Title Page   Next Page

Sep Oct Nov Dec Jan Feb March April May June

Use the **text tool** to type the months and instructions for the reader.

Use the **paintbrush tool** to make a small red dot for each event.

Add a Text Object for each event (see below).

Add 4 invisible Buttons around each clip art to hide and show the text objects (see below).

Add a Text Object for each event:

1 **Add a Text Object** next to one of the events on the timeline. Don't worry if it covers part of your timeline.

2 On the **Text Appearance** window, name the text object for the month that goes with it. Then, click OK.

3 Type in a description of the event in the text object.

4 Repeat Steps 1–3 for the other three events.

On December 20, we had a concert with the band and the choir. We performed works by Beethoven and Bach.

Dec

Add 4 Invisible Buttons with HideShow effect:

1 **Add an invisible Button** to surround both the clip art and the small dot on the timeline.

On the Computer

Class Yearbook

2 When the **Actions** window appears, choose **None of the Above** for **Places to Go**. For **Things to Do**, select **Play a sound** and choose a sound. Click OK.

3 Back at the **Actions** window, select **New Button Actions** under **Things to Do**. When the **New Button Actions** window appears, select **HideShow** under **Names**. Then, click **Use this NBA**. This window will appear:

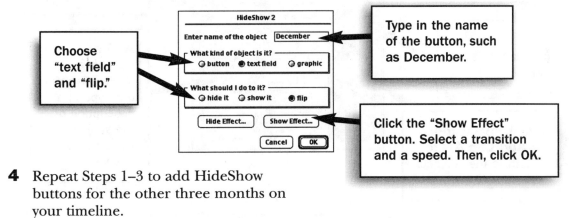

Choose "text field" and "flip."

Type in the name of the button, such as December.

Click the "Show Effect" button. Select a transition and a speed. Then, click OK.

HideShow 2

Enter name of the object   December

What kind of object is it?
○ button   ● text field   ○ graphic

What should I do to it?
○ hide it   ○ show it   ● flip

Hide Effect...   Show Effect...

Cancel   OK

4 Repeat Steps 1–3 to add HideShow buttons for the other three months on your timeline.

5 **Save Stack**.

CARD 5: FIELD TRIPS

Add a **non-scrolling** Text **Object** for the card title.

Add a **Button** that connects to Card 2.

Add a **non-scrolling** Text **Object** labeled "Hear our memories."

Use the **paint bucket tool** to fill in the background.

Add a **Button** that connects to next card.

Add a **Graphic Object** of a photo from a field trip.

Add **2 Buttons** that play a recording about the field trip.

IIS Proj#100.STK - Card 3

Title Page

The Explorers - Field Trips
St. Augustine

Next Page

HEAR OUR MEMORIES

SHARI

JORGE   JACK

TIFFANI   DARRAH

On the Computer

Class Yearbook

CARD 6: SUBJECTS

Add a **non-scrolling** **Text Object** for the card title.

Add a **Button** that connects to Card 2.

Use the **paint tools** or **Add Clip Art** to illustrate the subjects you studied.

Add a **Button** that connects to the next card.

Add a **scrolling** **Text Object** and type in a description of the subjects you studied this year.

The Explorers - Subjects

Title Page | Next Page

Here are four things we learned this year.
First, we learned how to use HyperStudio and make stacks or projects on the computer.
Second, in science we learned how to make a compost pile and the most important ingredient, WORMS! Also, Mr. Rustay taught us how to preserve dead animal bodies and put them in jars to observe

CARD 7: QUIZ

Add a **non-scrolling** **Text Object** for the card title.

Add a **Button** that connects to Card 2.

Add a **Button** that connects to the next card.

Use the **text tool** to type the question.

Add a **non-scrolling** **Text Object** for each answer choice (see below).

The Explorers - Quiz

Title Page | Next Page

Mr. Rustay likes to _____ .
This is really funny, but we try to avoid it. We need a brush afterwards.

a. drink "Diet Coke"

b. teach math and HyperStudio

c. mess up our hair

Add a Text Object for each answer choice:

1 Add a **Text Object**. Click on the **Actions** button. For **Places to Go**, select **None of the Above**. Under **Things to Do**, choose **Play a sound**.

2 On the **Tape Deck** window, record the response for the answer choice clicked. (See your Planning Pages.) Click OK, then click **Done** on the **Actions** window.

3 Repeat Steps 1–2 for the other two answer choices.

4 Save Stack.